THE WRITING LIFE

T0025734

BY THE SAME AUTHOR

The Maytrees

Mornings Like This

Modern American Memoirs

The Annie Dillard Reader

For the Time Being

The Living

An American Childhood

Encounters with Chinese Writers

Teaching a Stone to Talk

Living by Fiction

Holy the Firm

Pilgrim at Tinker Creek

Tickets for a Prayer Wheel

THE
WRITING
LIFE

ANNIE
DILLARD

HARPER ● PERENNIAL

NEW YORK ● LONDON ● TORONTO ● SYDNEY ● NEW DELHI ● AUCKLAND

Special thanks to: Ann Beattie, Marc Chenétier, Cody Rose Clevidence, Ophelia Dahl, Wendy Doniger, Tim Duggan, Paul Farmer, Amy Fields, Lewis Lapham, Will Lippincott, Allison Lorentzen, John Martini, Derek Parsons, Phyllis Rose, David Schorr, Timothy Seldes, Molly Simonds, Lee Smith, and Anne Warner.

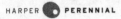 HARPER PERENNIAL

Excerpts from this book appeared in *Black Warrior Review*, *Esquire*, the *New York Times Book Review*, *Tikkun*, and *TriQuarterly*.

A hardcover edition of this book was published in 1989 by Harper & Row, Publishers, Inc.

THE WRITING LIFE. Copyright © 1989 by Annie Dillard. All rights reserved. Printed in the United States of America. No part of this book may be used or reproduced in any manner whatsoever without written permission except in the case of brief quotations embodied in critical articles and reviews. For information, address HarperCollins Publishers, 195 Broadway, New York, NY 10007.

HarperCollins books may be purchased for educational, business, or sales promotional use. For information, please e-mail the Special Markets Department at SPsales@harpercollins.com.

First Harper Perennial edition published 1990, reissued 1998 and 2013.

Designed by C. Linda Dingler

The Library of Congress has catalogued the hardcover edition as follows:

Dillard, Annie.
The writing life/Annie Dillard.—1st ed.
       p. cm.
ISBN 0-06-016516-6
1. Dillard, Annie—Biography. 2. Authors, American—20th century—
Biography. I. Title.
PS3554.I398Z478   1989
818'.5409—dc19
[B]   89-45034

ISBN 978-0-06-091988-7 (reissue)

24 25 26 27 28 LBC 78 77 76 75 74

For
BOB

THE WRITING LIFE

No one suspects the days to be gods. —EMERSON

Chapter One

Do not hurry; do not rest. —GOETHE

WHEN YOU WRITE, you lay out a line of words. The line of words is a miner's pick, a woodcarver's gouge, a surgeon's probe. You wield it, and it digs a path you follow. Soon you find yourself deep in new territory. Is it a dead end, or have you located the real subject? You will know tomorrow, or this time next year.

You make the path boldly and follow it fearfully. You go where the path leads. At the end of the path, you find a box canyon. You hammer out reports, dispatch bulletins.

The writing has changed, in your hands, and in a twinkling, from an expression of your notions to an epistemological tool. The new place interests you because it is not clear. You attend. In your humility, you lay down the words carefully, watching all the

angles. Now the earlier writing looks soft and care-
less. Process is nothing; erase your tracks. The path
is not the work. I hope your tracks have grown over;
I hope birds ate the crumbs; I hope you will toss it
all and not look back.

The line of words is a hammer. You hammer
against the walls of your house. You tap the walls,
lightly, everywhere. After giving many years' atten-
tion to these things, you know what to listen for.
Some of the walls are bearing walls; they have to
stay, or everything will fall down. Other walls can
go with impunity; you can hear the difference. Un-
fortunately, it is often a bearing wall that has to go.
It cannot be helped. There is only one solution,
which appalls you, but there it is. Knock it out.
Duck.

Courage utterly opposes the bold hope that this is
such fine stuff the work needs it, or the world. Cour-
age, exhausted, stands on bare reality: this writing
weakens the work. You must demolish the work and
start over. You can save some of the sentences, like
bricks. It will be a miracle if you can save some of
the paragraphs, no matter how excellent in them-
selves or hard-won. You can waste a year worrying
about it, or you can get it over with now. (Are you
a woman, or a mouse?)

The part you must jettison is not only the best-
written part; it is also, oddly, that part which was to
have been the very point. It is the original key pas-
sage, the passage on which the rest was to hang, and
from which you yourself drew the courage to begin.
Henry James knew it well, and said it best. In his

4

preface to *The Spoils of Poynton,* he pities the writer, in a comical pair of sentences that rises to a howl: "Which is the work in which he hasn't surrendered, under dire difficulty, the best thing he meant to have kept? In which indeed, before the dreadful *done,* doesn't he ask himself what has become of the thing all for the sweet sake of which it was to proceed to that extremity?"

So it is that a writer writes many books. In each book, he intended several urgent and vivid points, many of which he sacrificed as the book's form hardened. "The youth gets together his materials to build a bridge to the moon," Thoreau noted mournfully, "or perchance a palace or temple on the earth, and at length the middle-aged man concludes to build a wood-shed with them." The writer returns to these materials, these passionate subjects, as to unfinished business, for they are his life's work.

———

It is the beginning of a work that the writer throws away.

A painting covers its tracks. Painters work from the ground up. The latest version of a painting overlays earlier versions, and obliterates them. Writers, on the other hand, work from left to right. The discardable chapters are on the left. The latest version of a literary work begins somewhere in the work's middle, and hardens toward the end. The earlier version remains lumpishly on the left; the work's beginning greets the reader with the wrong hand. In those early pages and chapters anyone may find bold leaps to nowhere, read the brave beginnings of dropped themes, hear a tone since abandoned, discover blind alleys, track red herrings, and laboriously learn a setting now false.

Several delusions weaken the writer's resolve to throw away work. If he has read his pages too often, those pages will have a necessary quality, the ring of the inevitable, like poetry known by heart; they will perfectly answer their own familiar rhythms. He will retain them. He may retain those pages if they possess some virtues, such as power in themselves, though they lack the cardinal virtue, which is pertinence to, and unity with, the book's thrust. Sometimes the writer leaves his early chapters in place from gratitude; he cannot contemplate them or read them without feeling again the blessed relief that exalted him when the words first appeared—relief that he was writing anything at all. That beginning served to get him where he was going, after all; surely the reader needs it, too, as groundwork. But no.

Every year the aspiring photographer brought a stack of his best prints to an old, honored photographer, seeking his judgment. Every year the old man studied the prints and painstakingly ordered them into two piles, bad and good. Every year the old man moved a certain landscape print into the bad stack. At length he turned to the young man: "You submit this same landscape every year, and every year I put it on the bad stack. Why do you like it so much?" The young photographer said, "Because I had to climb a mountain to get it."

A cabdriver sang his songs to me, in New York. Some we sang together. He had turned the meter off; he drove around midtown, singing. One long song he sang twice; it was the only dull one. I said, You already sang that one; let's sing something else. And he said, "You don't know how long it took me to get that one together."

How many books do we read from which the writer lacked courage to tie off the umbilical cord? How many gifts do we open from which the writer neglected to remove the price tag? Is it pertinent, is it courteous, for us to learn what it cost the writer personally?

———

You write it all, discovering it at the end of the line of words. The line of words is a fiber optic, flexible as wire; it illumines the path just before its fragile tip. You probe with it, delicate as a worm.

———

Few sights are so absurd as that of an inchworm leading its dimwit life. Inchworms are the caterpillar larvae of several moths or butterflies. The cabbage looper, for example, is an inchworm. I often see an inchworm: it is a skinny bright green thing, pale and thin as a vein, an inch long, and apparently totally unfit for life in this world. It wears out its days in constant panic.

Every inchworm I have seen was stuck in long grasses. The wretched inchworm hangs from the side of a grassblade and throws its head around from side to side, seeming to wail. What! No further? Its back pair of nubby feet clasps the grass stem; its front three pairs of nubs rear back and flail in the air, apparently in search of a footing. What! No further? What? It searches everywhere in the wide world for the rest of the grass, which is right under its nose. By dumb luck it touches the grass. Its front legs hang on; it lifts and buckles its green inch, and places its hind legs just behind its front legs. Its body makes a loop, a bight. All it has to do now is slide its front legs up the grass stem. Instead it gets lost. It throws up its head and front legs, flings its upper body out into the void, and panics again. What! No further? End of world? And so forth, until it actually reaches the grasshead's tip. By then its wee weight may be bending the grass toward some other grass plant. Its davening, apocalyptic prayers sway the grasshead and bump it into something. I have seen it many times. The blind and frantic numbskull makes it off one grassblade and onto another one, which it will climb in virtual hysteria for several hours. Every step brings it to the universe's rim. And now— What! No further? End of world? Ah, here's ground. What! No further? Yike!

"Why don't you just jump?" I tell it, disgusted. "Put yourself out of your misery."

———

I admire those eighteenth-century Hasids who understood the risk of prayer. Rabbi Uri of Strelisk took sorrowful leave of his household every morning because he was setting off to his prayers. He told his family how to dispose of his manuscripts if praying should kill him. A ritual slaughterer, similarly, every morning bade goodbye to his wife and children and wept as if he would never see them again. His friend asked him why. Because, he answered, when I begin I call out to the Lord. Then I pray, "Have mercy on us." Who knows what the Lord's power will do to me in that moment after I have invoked it and before I beg for mercy?

When you are stuck in a book; when you are well into writing it, and know what comes next, and yet cannot go on; when every morning for a week or a month you enter its room and turn your back on it; then the trouble is either of two things. Either the structure has forked, so the narrative, or the logic, has developed a hairline fracture that will shortly split it up the middle—or you are approaching a fatal mistake. What you had planned will not do. If you pursue your present course, the book will explode or collapse, and you do not know about it yet, quite.

In Bridgeport, Connecticut, one morning in April 1987, a six-story concrete-slab building under construction collapsed, and killed twenty-eight men. Just before it collapsed, a woman across the street leaned from her window and said to a passerby, "That building is starting to shake." "Lady," he said, according to the Hartford *Courant,* "you got rocks in your head."

You notice only this: your worker—your one and only, your prized, coddled, and driven worker—is not going out on that job. Will not budge, not even for you, boss. Has been at it long enough to know when the air smells wrong; can sense a tremor through boot soles. Nonsense, you say; it is perfectly safe. But the worker will not go. Will not even look at the site. Just developed heart trouble. Would rather starve. Sorry.

What do you do? Acknowledge, first, that you cannot do nothing. Lay out the structure you already have, x-ray it for a hairline fracture, find it, and think about it for a week or a year; solve the insoluble problem. Or subject the next part, the part at which the worker balks, to harsh tests. It harbors an unexamined and wrong premise. Something completely necessary is false or fatal. Once you find it, and if you can accept the finding, of course it will mean starting again. This is why many experienced writers urge young men and women to learn a useful trade.

———

Every morning you climb several flights of stairs, enter your study, open the French doors, and slide your desk and chair out into the middle of the air. The desk and chair float thirty feet from the ground, between the crowns of maple trees. The furniture is in place; you go back for your thermos of coffee. Then, wincing, you step out again through the French doors and sit down on the chair and look over the desktop. You can see clear to the river from here in winter. You pour yourself a cup of coffee.

Birds fly under your chair. In spring, when the leaves open in the maples' crowns, your view stops in the treetops just beyond the desk; yellow warblers hiss and whisper on the high twigs, and catch flies. Get to work. Your work is to keep cranking the flywheel that turns the gears that spin the belt in the engine of belief that keeps you and your desk in midair.

————

Putting a book together is interesting and exhilarating. It is sufficiently difficult and complex that it engages all your intelligence. It is life at its most free. Your freedom as a writer is not freedom of expression in the sense of wild blurting; you may not let rip. It is life at its most free, if you are fortunate enough to be able to try it, because you select your materials, invent your task, and pace yourself. In the democracies, you may even write and publish anything you please about any governments or institutions, even if what you write is demonstrably false.

The obverse of this freedom, of course, is that your work is so meaningless, so fully for yourself alone, and so worthless to the world, that no one except you cares whether you do it well, or ever. You are free to make several thousand close judgment calls a day. Your freedom is a by-product of your days' triviality. A shoe salesman—who is doing others' tasks, who must answer to two or three bosses, who must do his job their way, and must put himself in their hands, at their place, during their hours—is nevertheless working usefully. Further, if the shoe salesman fails to appear one morning, someone will notice and miss him. Your manuscript, on which you lavish such care, has no needs or wishes; it knows you not. Nor does anyone need your manuscript; everyone needs shoes more. There are many manuscripts already—worthy ones, most edifying and moving ones, intelligent and powerful ones. If you believed *Paradise Lost* to be excellent, would you buy it? Why not shoot yourself, actually, rather than finish one more excellent manuscript on which to gag the world?

———

To find a honey tree, first catch a bee. Catch a bee when its legs are heavy with pollen; then it is ready for home. It is simple enough to catch a bee on a flower: hold a cup or glass above the bee, and when it flies up, cap the cup with a piece of cardboard. Carry the bee to a nearby open spot—best an elevated one—release it, and watch where it goes. Keep your eyes on it as long as you can see it, and hie you to that last known place. Wait there until you see another bee; catch it, release it, and watch. Bee after bee will lead toward the honey tree, until you see the final bee enter the tree. Thoreau describes this process in his journals. So a book leads its writer.

You may wonder how you start, how you catch the first one. What do you use for bait?

You have no choice. One bad winter in the Arctic, and not too long ago, an Algonquin woman and her baby were left alone after everyone else in their winter camp had starved. Ernest Thompson Seton tells it. The woman walked from the camp where everyone had died, and found at a lake a cache. The cache contained one small fishhook. It was simple to rig a line, but she had no bait, and no hope of bait. The baby cried. She took a knife and cut a strip from her own thigh. She fished with the worm of her own flesh and caught a jackfish; she fed the child and herself. Of course she saved the fish gut for bait. She lived alone at the lake, on fish, until spring, when she walked out again and found people. Seton's informant had seen the scar on her thigh.

———

To comfort friends discouraged by their writing pace, you could offer them this:

It takes years to write a book—between two and ten years. Less is so rare as to be statistically insignificant. One American writer has written a dozen major books over six decades. He wrote one of those books, a perfect novel, in three months. He speaks of it, still, with awe, almost whispering. Who wants to offend the spirit that hands out such books?

Faulkner wrote *As I Lay Dying* in six weeks; he claimed he knocked it off in his spare time from a twelve-hour-a-day job performing manual labor. There are other examples from other continents and centuries, just as albinos, assassins, saints, big people, and little people show up from time to time in large populations. Out of a human population on earth of four and a half billion, perhaps twenty people can write a serious book in a year. Some people lift cars, too. Some people enter week-long sled-dog races, go over Niagara Falls in barrels, fly planes through the Arc de Triomphe. Some people feel no pain in childbirth. Some people eat cars. There is no call to take human extremes as norms.

———

Graham Greene noticed that since a novel "takes perhaps years to write, the author is not the same man at the end of the book as he was at the beginning . . . as though [the novel] were something he had begun in childhood and was finishing now in old age." The long poem, John Berryman said, takes between five and ten years. Thomas Mann was a prodigy of production. Working full time, he wrote a page a day. That is 365 pages a year, for he did write every day—a good-sized book a year. At a page a day, he was one of the most prolific literary writers who ever lived. Flaubert wrote steadily, with only the usual, appalling, strains. For twenty-five years he finished a big book every five to seven years. If a full-time writer averages a book every five years, that makes seventy-three usable pages a year, or a usable fifth of a page a day. The years that biographers and other nonfiction writers spend amassing and mastering materials match the years novelists and short story writers spend fabricating solid worlds that answer to immaterial truths. On plenty of days the writer can write three or four pages, and on plenty of other days he concludes he must throw them away. These truths comfort the anguished. They do not mean, by any means, that faster-written books are worse books.

They just mean that most writers might well stop berating themselves for writing at a normal, slow pace.

Octavio Paz cites the example of "Saint-Pol Roux, who used to hang the inscription 'The poet is working' from his door while he slept."

The notion that one can write better during one season of the year than another Samuel Johnson labeled, "Imagination operating upon luxury." Another luxury for an idle imagination is the writer's own feeling about the work. There is neither a proportional relationship, nor an inverse one, between a writer's estimation of a work in progress and its actual quality. The feeling that the work is magnificent, and the feeling that it is abominable, are both mosquitoes to be repelled, ignored, or killed, but not indulged.

The reason to perfect a piece of prose as it progresses—to secure each sentence before building on it—is that original writing fashions a form. It unrolls out into nothingness. It grows cell to cell, bole to bough to twig to leaf; any careful word may suggest a route, may begin a strand of metaphor or event out of which much, or all, will develop. Perfecting the work inch by inch, writing from the first word toward the last, displays the courage and fear this method induces. The strain, like Giacometti's penciled search for precision and honesty, enlivens the work and impels it toward its truest end. A pile of decent work behind him, no matter how small, fuels the writer's hope, too; his pride emboldens and impels him. One Washington writer—Charlie Butts—so prizes momentum, and so fears self-consciousness, that he writes fiction in a rush of his own devising. He leaves his house on distracting errands, hurries in the door, and without taking off his coat, sits at a typewriter and retypes in a blur of speed all of the story he has written to date. Impetus propels him to add another sentence or two before he notices he is writing and seizes up. Then he leaves the house and repeats the process; he runs in the door and retypes the entire story, hoping to squeeze out another sentence the way some car engines turn over after the ignition is off, or the way Warner Bros.' Wile E. Coyote continues running for several yards beyond the edge of a cliff, until he notices.

The reason not to perfect a work as it progresses is that, concomitantly, original work fashions a form the true shape of which it discovers only as it proceeds, so the early strokes are useless, however fine their sheen. Only when a paragraph's role in the context of the whole work is clear can the envisioning writer direct its complexity of detail to strengthen the work's ends.

Fiction writers who toss up their arms helplessly because their characters "take over"—powerful rascals, what is a god to do?—refer, I think, to these structural mysteries that seize any serious work, whether or not it possesses fifth-column characters who wreak havoc from within. Sometimes part of a book simply gets up and walks away. The writer cannot force it back in place. It wanders off to die. It is like the astonishing—and common—starfish called the sea star. A sea star is a starfish with many arms;

each arm is called a ray. From time to time a sea star breaks itself, and no one knows why. One of the rays twists itself off and walks away. Dr. S. P. Monks describes one species, which lives on rocky Pacific shores:

"I am inclined to think that *Phataria* . . . always breaks itself, no matter what may be the impulse. They make breaks when conditions are changed, sometimes within a few hours after being placed in jars. . . . Whatever may be the stimulus, the animal can and does break of itself. . . . The ordinary method is for the main portion of the starfish to remain fixed and passive with the tube feet set on the side of the departing ray, and for this ray to walk slowly away at right angles to the body, to change position, twist, and do all the active labor necessary to the breakage." Marine biologist Ed Ricketts comments on this: "It would seem that in an animal that deliberately pulls itself apart we have the very acme of something or other."

———

The written word is weak. Many people prefer life to it. Life gets your blood going, and it smells good. Writing is mere writing, literature is mere. It appeals only to the subtlest senses—the imgination's vision, and the imagination's hearing—and the moral sense, and the intellect. This writing that you do, that so thrills you, that so rocks and exhilarates you, as if you were dancing next to the band, is barely audible to anyone else. The reader's ear must adjust down from loud life to the subtle, imaginary sounds of the written word. An ordinary reader picking up a book can't yet hear a thing; it will take half an hour to pick up the writing's modulations, its ups and downs and louds and softs.

An intriguing entomological experiment shows that a male butterfly will ignore a living female butterfly of his own species in favor of a painted cardboard one, if the cardboard one is big. If the cardboard one is bigger than he is, bigger than any female butterfly ever could be. He jumps the piece of cardboard Over and over again, he jumps the piece of cardboard. Nearby, the real, living female butterfly opens and closes her wings in vain.

Films and television stimulate the body's senses too, in big ways. A nine-foot handsome face, and its three-foot-wide smile, are irresistible. Look at the long legs on that man, as high as a wall, and coming straight toward you. The music builds. The moving, lighted screen fills your brain. You do not like filmed car chases? See if you can turn away. Try not to watch. Even knowing you are manipulated, you are still as helpless as the male butterfly drawn to painted cardboard.

That is the movies. That is their ground. The printed word cannot compete with the movies on their ground, and should not. You can describe beautiful faces, car chases, or valleys full of Indians on horseback until you run out of words, and you will not approach the movies' spectacle. Novels written with film contracts in mind have a faint but unmistakable, and ruinous, odor. I cannot name what, in the text, alerts the reader to suspect the writer of mixed motives; I cannot specify which sentences, in several books, have caused me to read on with increasing dismay, and finally close the books because I smelled a rat. Such books seem uneasy being books; they seem eager to fling off their disguises and jump onto screens.

Why would anyone read a book instead of watching big people move on a screen? Because a book can be literature. It is a subtle thing—a poor thing, but our own. In my view, the more literary the book—the more purely verbal, crafted sentence by sentence, the more imaginative, reasoned, and deep—the more likely people are to read it. The people who read are the people who like literature, after all, whatever that might be. They like, or require, what books alone have. If they want to see films that evening, they will find films. If they do not like to read, they will not. People who read are not too lazy to flip on the television; they prefer books. I cannot imagine a sorrier pursuit than struggling for years to write a book that attempts to appeal to people who do not read in the first place.

———

You climb a long ladder until you can see over the roof, or over the clouds. You are-writing a book. You watch your shod feet step on each round rung, one at a time; you do not hurry and do not rest. Your feet feel the steep ladder's balance; the long muscles in your thighs check its sway. You climb steadily, doing your job in the dark. When you reach the end, there is nothing more to climb. The sun hits you. The bright wideness surprises you; you had forgotten there was an end. You look back at the ladder's two feet on the distant grass, astonished.

———

The line of words fingers your own heart. It invades arteries, and enters the heart on a flood of breath; it presses the moving rims of thick valves; it palpates the dark muscle strong as horses, feeling for something, it knows not what. A queer picture beds in the muscle like a worm encysted—some film of feeling, some song forgotten, a scene in a dark bedroom, a corner of the woodlot, a terrible dining room, that exalting sidewalk; these fragments are heavy with meaning. The line of words peels them back, dissects them out. Will the bared tissue burn? Do you want to expose these scenes to the light? You may locate them and leave them, or poke the spot hard till the sore bleeds on your finger, and write with that blood. If the sore spot is not fatal, if it does not grow and block something, you can use its power for many years, until the heart resorbs it.

The line of words feels for cracks in the firmament. The line of words is heading out past Jupiter this morning. Traveling 150 kilometers a second, it makes no sound. The big yellow planet and its white moons spin. The line of words speeds past Jupiter and its cumbrous, dizzying orbit; it looks neither to the right nor to the left. It will be leaving the solar system soon, single-minded, rapt, rushing heaven like a soul. You are in Houston, Texas, watching the monitor. You saw a simulation: the line of words waited still, hushed, pointed with longing. The big yellow planet spun toward it like a pitched ball and passed beside it, low and outside. Jupiter was so large, the arc of its edge at the screen's bottom looked flat. The probe twined on; its wild path passed between white suns small as dots; these stars fell away on either side, like the lights on a tunnel's walls.

Now you watch symbols move on your monitor; you stare at the signals the probe sends back, transmits in your own tongue, numbers. Maybe later you can guess at what they mean—what they might mean about space at the edge of the solar system, or about your instruments. Right now, you are flying. Right now, your job is to hold your breath.

Chapter Two

*What if the man could see Beauty Itself, pure,
unalloyed, stripped of mortality and all its
pollution, stains, and vanities, unchanging,
divine, . . . the man becoming, in that communion,
the friend of God, himself immortal; . . . would
that be a life to disregard?* —PLATO

I WRITE THIS in the most recent of my many studies—a pine shed on Cape Cod. The pine lumber is unfinished inside the study; the pines outside are finished trees. I see the pines from my two windows. Nuthatches spiral around their long, coarse trunks. Sometimes in June a feeding colony of mixed warblers flies through the pines; the warblers make a racket that draws me out the door. The warblers drift loosely through the stiff pine branches, and I follow through the thin long grass between the trunks.

The study—sold as a prefabricated toolshed—is eight feet by ten feet. Like a plane's cockpit, it is crammed bulkhead to bulkhead with high-tech equipment. All it needs is an altimeter; I never quite know where I am. There is a computer, a printer, and a photocopying machine. My backless chair, a prie-dieu on which I kneel, slides under the desk; I give it a little kick when I leave. There is an air conditioner, a heater, and an electric kettle. There is a low-tech bookshelf, a shelf of gull and whale bones, and a bed. Under the bed I stow paints—a one-pint can of yellow to touch up the windows' trim, and five or six tubes of artists' oils. The study affords ample room for one. One who is supposed to be writing books. You can read in the space of a coffin, and you can write in the space of a toolshed meant for mowers and spades.

I walk up here from the house every morning. The study and its pines, and the old summer cottages nearby, and the new farm just north of me, rise from an old sand dune high over a creeky salt marsh. From the bright lip of the dune I can see oyster farmers working their beds on the tide flats and sailboats under way in the saltwater bay. After I have warmed myself standing at the crest of the dune, I return under the pines, enter the study, slam the door so the latch catches—and then I cannot see. The green spot in front of my eyes outshines everything in the shade. I lie on the bed and play with a bird bone until I can see it.

Appealing workplaces are to be avoided. One wants a room with no view, so imagination can meet memory in the dark. When I furnished this study seven years ago, I pushed the long desk against a blank wall, so I could not see from either window. Once, fifteen years ago, I wrote in a cinder-block cell over a parking lot. It overlooked a tar-and-gravel roof. This pine shed under trees is not quite so good as the cinder-block study was, but it will do.

"The beginning of wisdom," according to a West African proverb, "is to get you a roof."

———

It was on summer nights in Roanoke, Virginia, that I wrote the second half of a book, *Pilgrim at Tinker Creek*. (I wrote the first half in the spring, at home.) Ruefully I noted then that I would possibly look back on those times as an idyll. I vowed to remember the difficulties. I have forgotten them now, however, and look back on those times as an idyll.

I slept until noon, as did my husband, who was also writing. I wrote once in the afternoon, and once again after our early dinner and a walk. During those months, I subsisted on that dinner, coffee, Coke, chocolate milk, and Vantage cigarettes. I worked till midnight, one, or two. When I came home in the middle of the night I was tired; I longed for a tolerant giant, a person as big as a house, to hold me and rock me. In fact, an exhausted day-dream—almost a hallucination—of being rocked and soothed sometimes forced itself upon me, and interrupted me even when I was talking or reading.

I had a room—a study carrel—in the Hollins College library, on the second floor. It was this room that overlooked a tar-and-gravel roof. A plate-glass window, beside me on the left, gave out onto the roof, a parking lot, a distant portion of Carvin Creek, some complicated Virginia sky, and a far hilltop where six cows grazed around a ruined foundation under red cedars.

From my desk I kept an eye out. Intriguing people, people I knew, pulled into the parking lot and climbed from their cars. The cows moved on the hilltop. (I drew the cows, for they were made interestingly; they hung in catenary curves from their skeletons, like two-man tents.) On the flat roof just outside the window, sparrows pecked gravel. One of the sparrows lacked a leg; one was missing a foot. If I stood and peered around, I could see a feeder creek run at the edge of a field. In the creek, even from that great distance, I could see muskrats and snapping turtles. If I saw a snapping turtle, I ran downstairs and out of the library to watch it or poke it.

One afternoon I made a pen drawing of the window and the landscape it framed. I drew the window's aluminum frame and steel hardware; I laid in the clouds, and the far hilltop with its ruined foundation and wandering cows. I outlined the parking lot and its tall row of mercury-vapor lights; I drew the cars, and the graveled rooftop foreground.

———

If I craned my head, I could see a grassy playing field below. One afternoon I peered around at that field and saw a softball game. Since I happened to have my fielder's glove with me in my study, I thought it would be the generous thing to join the game. On the field, I learned there was a music camp on campus for two weeks. The little boys playing softball were musical whizzes. They could not all play ball, but their patter was a treat. "All right, Macdonald," they jeered when one kid came to bat, "that pizzicato won't help you now." It was slightly better than no softball, so I played with them every day, second base, terrified that I would bust a prodigy's fingers on a throw to first or the plate.

I shut the blinds one day for good. I lowered the venetian blinds and flattened the slats. Then, by lamplight, I taped my drawing to the closed blind. There, on the drawing, was the window's view: cows, parking lot, hilltop, and sky. If I wanted a sense of the world, I could look at the stylized outline drawing. If I had possessed the skill, I would have painted, directly on the slats of the lowered blind, in meticulous colors, a *trompe l'oeil* mural view of all that the blinds hid. Instead, I wrote it.

———

On the Fourth of July, my husband and our friends drove into the city, Roanoke, to see the fireworks. I begged off; I wanted to keep working. I was working hard, although of course it did not seem hard enough at the time—a finished chapter every few weeks. I castigated myself daily for writing too slowly. Even when passages seemed to come easily, as though I were copying from a folio held open by smiling angels, the manuscript revealed the usual signs of struggle—bloodstains, teethmarks, gashes, and burns.

This night, as on most nights, I entered the library at dusk. The building was locked and dark. I had a key. Every night I let myself in, climbed the stairs, found my way between the tall stacks in the dark, located and unlocked my study's door, and turned on the light. I remembered how many stacks I had to hit with my hand in the dark before I turned down the row to my study. Even if I left only to get a drink of water, I felt and counted the stacks with my hand again to find my room. Once, in daylight, I glanced at a book on a stack's corner, a book I presumably touched every night with my hand. The book was *The World I Live In,* by Helen Keller. I read it at once: it surprised me by its strong and original prose.

When I flicked on my carrel light, there it all was: the bare room with yellow cinder-block walls; the big, flattened venetian blind and my drawing taped to it; two or three quotations taped up on index cards; and on a far table some ever-changing books, the fielder's mitt, and a yellow bag of chocolate-covered peanuts. There was the long, blond desk and its chair, and on the desk a dozen different-colored pens, some big index cards in careful, splayed piles, and my messy yellow legal pads. As soon as I saw that desktop, I remembered the task: the chapter, its problems, its phrases, its points.

This night I was concentrating on the chapter. The horizon of my consciousness was the contracted circle of yellow light inside my study—the lone lamp in the enormous, dark library. I leaned over the desk. I worked by hand. I doodled deliriously in the legal-pad margins. I fiddled with the index cards. I reread a sentence maybe a hundred times, and if I kept it I changed it seven or eight times, often substantially.

Now a June bug was knocking at my window. I was wrestling inside a sentence. I must have heard it a dozen times before it registered—before I noticed that I had been hearing a bug knock for half an hour. It made a hollow, bonking sound. Some people call the same fumbling, heavy insects "May beetles." It must have been attracted to my light— what little came between the slats of the blind. I dislike June bugs. Back to work. Knock again, knock again, and finally, to learn what monster of a fat, brown June bug could fly up to a second story and thump so insistently at my window as though it wanted admittance—at last, unthinkingly, I parted the venetian blind slats with my fingers, to look out.

And there were the fireworks, far away. It was the Fourth of July. I had forgotten. They were red and yellow, blue and green and white; they blossomed high in the black sky many miles away. The fireworks seemed as distant as the stars, but I could hear the late banging their bursting made. The sound, those bangs so muffled and out of sync, accompanied at random the silent, far sprays of color widening and raining down. It was the Fourth of July, and I had forgotten all of wide space and all of historical time. I opened the blinds a crack like eyelids, and it all came exploding in on me at once—oh yes, the world.

———

I have been looking into schedules. Even when we read physics, we inquire of each least particle,

What then shall I do this morning? How we spend our days is, of course, how we spend our lives. What we do with this hour, and that one, is what we are doing. A schedule defends from chaos and whim. It is a net for catching days. It is a scaffolding on which a worker can stand and labor with both hands at sections of time. A schedule is a mock-up of reason and order—willed, faked, and so brought into being; it is a peace and a haven set into the wreck of time; it is a lifeboat on which you find yourself, decades later, still living. Each day is the same, so you remember the series afterward as a blurred and powerful pattern.

The most appealing daily schedule I know is that of a turn-of-the-century Danish aristocrat. He got up at four and set out on foot to hunt black grouse, wood grouse, woodcock, and snipe. At eleven he met his friends, who had also been out hunting alone all morning. They converged "at one of these babbling brooks," he wrote. He outlined the rest of his schedule. "Take a quick dip, relax with a schnapps and a sandwich, stretch out, have a smoke, take a nap or just rest, and then sit around and chat until three. Then I hunt some more until sundown, bathe again, put on white tie and tails to keep up appearances, eat a huge dinner, smoke a cigar and sleep like a log until the sun comes up again to redden the eastern sky. This is living. . . . Could it be more perfect?"

There is no shortage of good days. It is good lives that are hard to come by. A life of good days lived in the senses is not enough. The life of sensation is the life of greed; it requires more and more. The life of the spirit requires less and less; time is ample and its passage sweet. Who would call a day spent reading a good day? But a life spent reading—that is a good life. A day that closely resembles every other day of the past ten or twenty years does not suggest itself as a good one. But who would not call Pasteur's life a good one, or Thomas Mann's?

Wallace Stevens in his forties, living in Hartford, Connecticut, hewed to a productive routine. He rose at six, read for two hours, and walked another hour—three miles—to work. He dictated poems to his secretary. He ate no lunch; at noon he walked for another hour, often to an art gallery. He walked home from work—another hour. After dinner he retired to his study; he went to bed at nine. On Sundays, he walked in the park. I don't know what he did on Saturdays. Perhaps he exchanged a few words with his wife, who posed for the Liberty dime. (One would rather read these people, or lead their lives, than be their wives. When the Danish aristocrat Wilhelm Dinesen shot birds all day, drank schnapps, napped, and dressed for dinner, he and his wife had three children under three. The middle one was Karen.)

Like Stevens, Osip Mandelstam composed poetry on the hoof. So did Dante. Nietzsche, like Emerson, took two long walks a day. "When my creative energy flowed most freely, my muscular activity was always greatest. . . . I might often have been seen dancing; I used to walk through the hills for seven or eight hours on end without a hint of fatigue; I slept well, laughed a good deal—I was perfectly vigorous and patient." On the other hand, A. E. Housman, almost predictably, maintained, "I have seldom written poetry unless I was rather out of health." This makes sense too, because writing a book, you can be too well for your own good.

Jack London claimed to write twenty hours a day. Before he undertook to write, he obtained the University of California course list and all the syllabi; he spent a year reading the textbooks in philosophy and literature. In subsequent years, once he had a book of his own under way, he set his alarm to wake him after four hours' sleep. Often he slept through the alarm, so, by his own account, he rigged it to drop a weight on his head. I cannot say I believe this, though a novel like *The Sea-Wolf* is strong evidence that some sort of weight fell on his head with some sort of frequency—but you wouldn't think a man would claim credit for it. London maintained that every writer needed a technique, experience, and a philosophical position. Perhaps the position need not be an airtight one; London himself felt comfortable with a weird amalgam of Karl Marx and Herbert Spencer (Marks & Sparks).

———

My working the graveyard shift in Virginia affected the book. It was a nature book full of sunsets; it wholly lacked dawns, and even mornings.

I was reading, among other things, Hasidism. If you stay awake one hundred nights, you get the vision of Elijah—the same revelation, earthquake and all. I was not eager for it, although it seemed to be just around the corner. I preferred this: "Rebbe Shmelke of Nickolsburg, it was told, never really heard his teacher, the Maggid of Mezritch, finish a thought because as soon as the latter would say 'and the Lord spoke,' Shmelke would begin shouting in wonderment, 'The Lord spoke, the Lord spoke,' and continue shouting until he had to be carried from the room."

The second floor of the library, where I worked every night, housed the rare-book room. It was a wide, carpeted, well-furnished room. On an end table, as if for decoration, stood a wooden chess set.

One night, stuck on an intractable problem in the writing, I wandered the dark library seeking distraction. I flicked on the lights in the rare-book room and looked at some of the books. I saw the chess set and moved white's king's pawn. I turned off the light and wandered back to my carrel.

A few nights later, I glanced into the rare-book room, and walked in, for black's queen's pawn had moved. I moved out my knight.

Every day, my unseen opponent moved. I moved. I never saw anyone anywhere near the rare-book room. The college was not in session; almost no one was around. Late at night I heard the night watchmen clank around downstairs in the dark. The watchmen never came upstairs. There was no one upstairs but me.

When the chess game was ten days old, I entered the rare-book room to find black's pieces coming toward me on the carpet. They seemed to be marching, in rows of two. I put them back as they had been, and made my move. The next day, the pieces were all pied on the board. I put them back as they had been. The next day, black had moved, rather brilliantly.

Late one night, while all this had been going on, and while the library was dark and locked as it had been all summer, and I had accustomed myself to the eeriness of it, I left my carrel to cross the darkness and get a drink of water. I saw a strange chunk of light on the floor between stacks. Passing the stacks, I saw the light spread across the hall. I held my breath. The light was coming from the rare-book room; the door was open.

I approached quietly, and looked in the room from an angle. There, at the chess table, stood a baby. The baby had blond curls and was wearing only a diaper.

I paused, considering that I had been playing a reasonable game of chess for two weeks with a naked baby. After a while I could make out the sound of voices; I moved closer to the doorway and peered in. There was the young head librarian and his wife, sitting on chairs. I pieced together the rest of it. The librarian stopped by to pick something up. Naturally, he had a key. The couple happened to have the baby along. The baby, just learning to walk, had cruised from the chairs to the table. The baby was holding on to the table, not studying the chess pieces' positions. I greeted the family and played with the baby until they left.

I never did learn who or what was playing chess

with me. The game went on until my lunatic oppo-
nent scrambled the board so violently the game was
over.

———

During that time, I let all the houseplants die.
After the book was finished I noticed them; the
plants hung completely black dead in their pots in
the bay window. For I had not only let them die, I
had not moved them. During that time, I told all my
out-of-town friends they could not visit for a while.

"I understand you're married," a man said to me
at a formal lunch in New York my publisher had
arranged. "How do you have time to write a book?"

Sir?

"Well," he said, "you have to have a garden, for
instance. You have to entertain." And I thought he
was foolish, this man in his seventies, who had no
idea what you must do. But the fanaticism of my
twenties shocks me now. As I feared it would.

Chapter Three

Another day, another dollar;
fourteen hours on snowshoes and wish I had pie.
—FROM A MAINE TRAPPER'S DIARY

ONCE, in order to finish a book I was writing and yet not live in the same room with it, I begged a cabin to use as a study. I finished the book there, wrote some other things, and learned to split wood. All this was on a remote and sparsely populated island on Haro Strait, where I moved when I left Virginia. The island was in northern Puget Sound, Washington State, across the water from Canadian islands.

The cabin was a single small room near the water. Its walls were shrunken planks, not insulated; in January, February, and March, it was cold. There were two small metal beds in the room, two cupboards, some shelves over a little counter, a wood stove, and a table under a window, where I wrote. The window looked out on a bit of sandflat overgrown with thick, varicolored mosses; there were a few small firs where the sandflat met the cobble beach; and there was the water: Puget Sound, and all the sky over it and all the other wild islands in the distance under the sky. It was very grand. But you get used to it. I don't much care where I work. I don't notice things. The door used to blow open and startle me witless. I did, however, notice the cold.

I tried to heat the cabin with the wood stove and a kerosene heater, but I never was warm. I used to work wearing a wool cap, long wool tights, sweaters, a down jacket, and a scarf. I was too lazy to stick a damper in the wood stove chimney; I kept putting off the task for a warm day. Thoreau said that his firewood warmed him twice—because he labored to cut his own. Mine froze me twice, for the same reason. After I learned to split wood, in a manner I am shortly to relate—after I learned to split wood, I stepped out into the brute northeaster and split just enough alder to last me through working hours, which was not enough splitting to warm me. Then I came in and kindled a fire in the stove, all the heat of which vanished up the chimney.

At first, in the good old days, I did not know how to split wood. I set a chunk of alder on the chopping block and harassed it, at enormous exertion, into tiny wedges that flew all over the sandflat and lost themselves. What I did was less like splitting wood than chipping flints. After a few whacks my alder chunk still stood serene and unmoved, its base untouched, its tip a thorn. And then I actually tried to turn the sorry thing over and balance it on its wee head while I tried to chop its feet off before it fell over. God save us.

All this was a very warm process. I removed my down jacket, my wool hat and scarf. Alas, those early wood-splitting days, when I truly warmed myself, didn't last long. I lost the knack.

I did not know it at the time, but during those first weeks when I attacked my wood every morning, I was collecting a crowd—or what passed on the island for a crowd. At the sound of my ax, Doe and Bob—real islanders, proper, wood-splitting islanders—paused in their activities and mustered, unseen, across the sandflat, under the firs. They were watching me (oh, the idleness) try to split wood. It must have been a largely silent comedy. Later, when they confessed, and I railed at them, Bob said innocently that the single remark he had ever permitted himself had been, "I love to watch Annie split wood."

One night, while all this had been going on, I had a dream in which I was given to understand, by the powers that be, how to split wood. You aim, said the dream—of course!—at the chopping block. It is true. You aim at the chopping block, not at the wood; then you split the wood, instead of chipping it. You cannot do the job cleanly unless you treat the wood as the transparent means to an end, by aiming past it. But then, alas, you easily split your day's wood in a few minutes, in the freezing cold, without working up any heat; then you utterly forfeit your only chance of getting warm.

The knack of splitting wood was the only useful

thing I had ever learned from any dream, and my attitude toward the powers that be was not entirely grateful. The island comedy was over; everybody had to go back to work; and I never did get warm.

————

Much has been written about the life of the mind. I find the phrase itself markedly dreamy. The mind of the writer does indeed do something before it dies, and so does its owner, but I would be hard put to call it living.

It should surprise no one that the life of the writer—such as it is—is colorless to the point of sensory deprivation. Many writers do little else but sit in small rooms recalling the real world. This explains why so many books describe the author's childhood. A writer's childhood may well have been the occasion of his only firsthand experience. Writers read literary biography, and surround themselves with other writers, deliberately to enforce in themselves the ludicrous notion that a reasonable option for occupying yourself on the planet until your life span plays itself out is sitting in a small room for the duration, in the company of pieces of paper.

Inside the small room, the writer is deeply preoccupied with things hitherto undreamed of. He finds himself inventing wholly new techniques in the service of his art.

Once, for instance, I had an office in the halls of a university English department, which was of course deserted nights and weekends. There I began writing a terrifically abstract book of literary and aesthetic theory. The kindly secretaries gave me a key to the faculty lounge so I could boil water for coffee at odd hours. The faculty lounge was around the corner and out of my earshot; it had a sink, a single stove burner, and a teakettle. The first night I used this arrangement I forgot all about the water I was boiling and scorched the kettle. It smelled terrible, and I confessed the next day. The secretaries said they would give me another chance.

It was an interesting kettle. Life is so interesting. It was a whistling kettle, but the secretaries did not want it to whistle, so they jammed the circular, perforated lid of an old percolator in its mouth. This aluminum lid became a hot item in the teeth of all that steam, so someone had devised a method of removing it with a springy wooden clothespin. Perhaps that same someone had carried the clothespin to the office for that purpose. Pretty soon people simply left the clothespin clamped on the aluminum percolator lid, which in turn jutted from the kettle's mouth. That is how things were when I got there.

After I burned the kettle, I had to discover a method to remind myself that I had water boiling on the stove in the faculty lounge, so I stuck the clothespin on my finger. It was, as it happened, a strong clothespin, and I had to move it every twenty seconds. This action, and the pain, kept me in the real world until the water actually boiled. This was the theory, and it worked. So that is how I wrote those nights, wrote a book about high holy art: moving a clothespin up and down my increasingly reddened little finger. Why people want to be writers I will never know, unless it is that their lives lack a material footing.

———

The materiality of the writer's life cannot be exaggerated. If you like metaphysics, throw pots. How fondly I recall thinking, in the old days, that to write you needed paper, pen, and a lap. How appalled I was to discover that, in order to write so much as a sonnet, you need a warehouse. You can easily get so confused writing a thirty-page chapter that in order to make an outline for the second draft, you have to rent a hall. I have often "written" with the mechanical aid of a twenty-foot conference table. You lay your pages along the table's edge and pace out the work. You walk along the rows; you weed bits, move bits, and dig out bits, bent over the rows with full hands like a gardener. After a couple of hours, you have taken an exceedingly dull nine-mile hike. You go home and soak your feet.

———

Remarkably material also is the writer's attempt to control his own energies so he can work. He must be sufficiently excited to rouse himself to the task at hand, and not so excited he cannot sit down to it. He must have faith sufficient to impel and renew the work, yet not so much faith he fancies he is writing well when he is not.

For writing a first draft requires from the writer a peculiar internal state which ordinary life does not induce. If you were a Zulu warrior banging on your shield with your spear for a couple of hours along with a hundred other Zulu warriors, you might be able to prepare yourself to write. If you were an Aztec maiden who knew months in advance that on a certain morning the priests were going to throw you into a hot volcano, and if you spent those months undergoing a series of purification rituals and drinking dubious liquids, you might, when the time came, be ready to write. But how, if you are neither Zulu warrior nor Aztec maiden, do you prepare yourself, all alone, to enter an extraordinary state on an ordinary morning?

How set yourself spinning? Where is an edge—a dangerous edge—and where is the trail to the edge and the strength to climb it?

———

Once I wrote a favorite, difficult book, a true account of three consecutive days on an island on the northwest coast. I began the book on one island and wrote most of it on another island; it took a long time. Much of it I wrote as poetry. Its two subjects were the relation of eternity to time and the problem of suffering innocents. The prose—once I decided to print it as prose—was so intense and accented, and the world it described was so charged with meaning, that the very thought of writing a word or two further made me tired. How could I add a sentence, or a paragraph, every day to this work I myself could barely understand? Its tone was fierce and exhilarated. Every time I looked at its part of the room, I got sleepy. I could not just pick up my shovel and walk to the mine. I could not add a word until I was ready, or that word would enfeeble or puncture the work.

On a ship near a coast, I had once seen a heavy-bodied moth panting. The moth stood on the ship's rail beside me and faced the water. It was a sphinx moth, a thick diurnal moth with tiny wings; people often mistake sphinx moths for hummingbirds. In order for them to fly at all, they must supercharge their flight muscles with oxygen. A resting state will not suffice. Beside me on the rail, the sphinx moth raced its engines for takeoff like a jet on a runway. I could see its brown body vibrate and its red-and-black wings tremble. I left its side to fetch drawing paper from my cabin. When I returned, it was still revving up.

Maybe I scared it. After trembling so violently that it seemed it must blow apart, the moth took flight. Its wings blurred, like a hummingbird's. It flew a few yards out over the water before it began losing altitude. It was going down. Its wings buzzed; it gained height and lost, gained and lost, and always lost more than it gained, until its heavy body dragged in the water, and it drowned before my eyes without a splash.

During some of the long, empty months at work on the book, I was living in a one-room log cabin on an empty beach. I had not yet borrowed the freezing cabin up the beach to use as a study; I did not yet know how foolish it was to plan days of solitary confinement, days in which my only activity was walking four or five feet from the bed to the desk. My husband wrote his book in another cabin; he worked much longer hours than I could. When my husband left after breakfast, I looked around the one-room cabin and out at the water and strip of beach. Nothing changed but the tides. Sometimes the empty beach was wide, and sometimes it was narrow. I could see it all from the bed, even on the darkest nights. The bed faced the beach and the water, and so did the desk; so did the table, and so did the sink. The whole house was a ship's rail. I turned to the work. This book interested me more passionately than any other. The task was to change intellectual passion to physical energy and some sort of narrative mastery, from a standing start.

———

"Bring on the lions!" I cried.

But there were no lions. I spent every day in the company of one dog and one cat whose every gesture emphasized that this was a day throughout whose duration intelligent creatures intended to sleep. I would have to crank myself up.

To crank myself up I stood on a jack and ran myself up. I tightened myself like a bolt. I inserted myself in a vise-clamp and wound the handle till the pressure built. I drank coffee in titrated doses. It was a tricky business, requiring the finely tuned judgment of a skilled anesthesiologist. There was a tiny range within which coffee was effective, short of which it was useless, and beyond which, fatal.

I pointed myself. I walked to the water. I played

the hateful recorder, washed dishes, drank coffee, stood on a beach log, watched bird. That was the first part; it could take all morning, or all month. Only the coffee counted, and I knew it. It was boiled Colombian coffee: raw grounds brought just to boiling in cold water and stirred. Now I smoked a cigarette or two and read what I wrote yesterday. What I wrote yesterday needed to be slowed down. I inserted words in one sentence and hazarded a new sentence. At once I noticed that I was writing—which, as the novelist Frederick Buechner noted, called for a break, if not a full-scale celebration.

On break, I usually read Conrad Aiken's poetry aloud. It was pure sound unencumbered by sense. If I ever caught a poem's sense by accident, I could never use that poem again. I often read the Senlin poems, and "Sea Holly." Some days I read part of any poetry anthology's index of first lines. The parallels sounded strong and suggestive. They could set me off, perhaps.

This morning, as on so many mornings, I lacked sufficient fuel for liftoff. I looked at the legal pad pages again. A new section must be begun in the book, and a place found to put it. I wrote four or five sentences on a gamble, smoked more to stimulate the brain or stop the heart, whichever came first, and reheated a fourth mug of coffee. After the first boiling, the grounds sink to the coffeepot's bottom. When you reheat it, you call it refried coffee. I already felt like the empty kettle on a hot burner, the thin kettle whose water had boiled away. The top of my stomach felt bruised or burned—was this how mustard gas tasted? I drank the fourth mug without looking at it, any more than you look at the needle in a doctor's hand.

Now, alas, I had cranked too far. I could no longer play the recorder; I would need a bugle. I would break a piano. What could I do around the cabin? There was no wood to split. There was something I needed to fix with a hacksaw, but I rejected the work as too fine. Why not adopt a baby, design a curriculum, go sailing?

The dog opened one eye, cocked it at me, and rolled it up before her lids closed. People should not feed moralistic animals. If they're so holy, where are their books? I was starving, but eating was out of the question. Nausea might temper this energy, but eating would kill it.

I read it again. Reading, I drew all over it. This was usual. Now my drawings tightened and darkened; I pressed them into the paper. They were digging through the paper and into the desk. Where next? I knew where next. It was within my possibilities. If only I could concentrate. I must quit. I was too young to be living at a desk. Many fine people were out there living, people whose consciences permitted them to sleep at night despite their not having written a decent sentence that day, or ever.

Let's dance. I could not draw the lamp any more; it was too little. I walked out on the beach unseeing and fell back in the door, sick, dead, dying. I heated a bowl of soup which I ate blinded by coffee and nicotine, unremembering. I returned to the papers and enclosed a paragraph in parentheses; it meant that tomorrow I would delete the few sentences I wrote today. Too many days of this, I thought, too many days of this.

———

I do not so much write a book as sit up with it, as with a dying friend. During visiting hours, I enter its room with dread and sympathy for its many disorders. I hold its hand and hope it will get better.

This tender relationship can change in a twinkling. If you skip a visit or two, a work in progress will turn on you.

A work in progress quickly becomes feral. It reverts to a wild state overnight. It is barely domesticated, a mustang on which you one day fastened a halter, but which now you cannot catch. It is a lion you cage in your study. As the work grows, it gets harder to control; it is a lion growing in strength. You must visit it every day and reassert your mastery over it. If you skip a day, you are, quite rightly, afraid to open the door to its room. You enter its room with bravura, holding a chair at the thing and shouting, "Simba!"

———

Living thus—with your lion tamer's chair, your ax, your conference table, and your clothespin—you may excite in your fellow man not curiosity but profound indifference. It is not my experience that society hates and fears the writer, or that society adulates the writer. Instead my experience is the common one, that society places the writer so far beyond the pale that society does not regard the writer at all.

Whenever an encounter between a writer of good will and a regular person of good will happens to touch on the subject of writing, each person discovers, dismayed, that good will is of no earthly use. The conversation cannot proceed. From such chastening encounters I have always learned far more than I intended.

Once, for example, I learned from a conversation with a neighbor that I had been living as it were in a fool's paragraph.

This neighbor, who crewed on a ferryboat, was one of the world's good, sane people. He was the local sheriff. He was an emergency medical technician, a volunteer fireman, a husband and father, and an unequaled contributor of witty remarks into the window of each car that rolled on and off the ferry. May his tribe increase.

One rainy day, this member of the real world gave me a ride home. I invited him in for a minute, and somehow all hell broke loose.

Politely, he asked me about my writing. Foolishly, not dreaming I was about to set my own world tumbling down about my ears, I said I hated to write. I said I would rather do anything else. He was amazed. He said, "That's like a guy who works in a factory all day, and hates it." Then I was amazed, for so it was. It was *just* like that. Why did I do it? I had never inquired. How had I let it creep up on me? Why wasn't I running a ferryboat, like sane people?

I hid my amazement as well as I could from both of us, and said that actually I avoided writing, and mostly what I did by way of work was fool around, and that for example that morning I had been breaking my brain trying to explain Whitehead to my journal. Why, he wanted to know, was I doing that? Again I stopped completely short; I could not imagine why on earth I was doing that. Why was I doing that?

But I rallied and mustered and said that the idea was to learn things; that you learn a thing and then as a matter of course you learn the next thing, and the next thing. . . . As I spoke he nodded precisely in the way that one nods at the utterances of the deranged. ". . . And then," I finished brightly, "you die!"

At this we exchanged a mutual and enormous smile. Still nodding and smiling in perfect agreement, we ended the visit and walked to the door.

———

A week later I had a visit so instructive that when it was over, and I had fully absorbed its lesson, I considered never opening my door again. This was a visit from children.

During the week after the ferryman's visit, I asked myself where my life had gone wrong. I was too far removed from the world. My work was too obscure, too symbolic, too intellectual. It was not available to people. Recently I had published a complex narrative essay about a moth's flying into a candle, which no one had understood but a Yale critic, and he had understood it exactly. I myself was trained as a critic. I was a critic writing for critics: was this what I had in mind?

One day, full of such thoughts, I tried to work and failed. After eight hours of watching helplessly while my own inane, manneristic doodles overstepped their margins and covered the pages I was supposed to be writing, I gave up. I decided to hate myself, to make popcorn and read. I had just sunk into the couch, the bowl of popcorn beside me, when I heard footsteps outside. It was two little neighborhood boys, Brad and Brian, who were seven and six. "Smells good in here," Brian said. So we ate the bowl of popcorn on the floor and talked. They played the harmonica; they played the recorder; they played the ukulele.

Then Brian got up and stood by my desk, on which there happened to be a pen drawing of a burning candle.

Brian said, "Is that the candle the moth flew into?"

I looked at him: WHAT?

He said, and I quote exactly, "Is that the candle the moth flew into, and his abdomen got stuck, and his head caught fire?"

WHAT? I said. WHAT? These little blue-jeaned kids were in the first grade. They came up to my pockets. Brad, on the floor, piped up, "I liked that story." Why, if I was sincere in anything, did it seem to console me to repeat to myself, "Oh well, he's older"?

Later, before they left, Brian made certain I understood that whatever sphere of discourse I fancied I shared with any interlocutor, I was wrong. Brian said (admiringly, I thought), "Did you *write* that story?" I started to answer, when he continued, "Or did you type it?"

———

Here is a fairly sober version of what happens in the small room between the writer and the work itself. It is similar to what happens between a painter and the canvas.

First you shape the vision of what the projected work of art will be. The vision, I stress, is no marvelous thing: it is the work's intellectual structure and aesthetic surface. It is a chip of mind, a pleasing intellectual object. It is a vision of the work, not of the world. It is a glowing thing, a blurred thing of beauty. Its structure is at once luminous and translucent; you can see the world through it. After you receive the initial charge of this imaginary object, you add to it at once several aspects, and incubate it most gingerly as it grows into itself.

Many aspects of the work are still uncertain, of course; you know that. You know that if you proceed you will change things and learn things, that the form will grow under your hands and develop new and richer lights. But that change will not alter the vision or its deep structures; it will only enrich it. You know that, and you are right.

But you are wrong if you think that in the actual writing, or in the actual painting, you are filling in the vision. You cannot fill in the vision. You cannot even bring the vision to light. You are wrong if you think that you can in any way take the vision and tame it to the page. The page is jealous and tyrannical; the page is made of time and matter; the page always wins. The vision is not so much destroyed, exactly, as it is, by the time you have finished, forgotten. It has been replaced by this changeling, this bastard, this opaque lightless chunky ruinous work.

Here is how it happens. The vision is, *sub specie aeternitatis,* a set of mental relationships, a coherent series of formal possibilities. In the actual rooms of time, however, it is a page or two of legal paper filled with words and questions; it is a terrible diagram, a few books' names in a margin, an ambiguous doodle, a corner folded down in a library book. These are memos from the thinking brain to witless hope.

Nevertheless, ignoring the provisional and pathetic nature of these scraps, and bearing the vision itself in mind—having it before your sights like the very Grail—you begin to scratch out the first faint marks on the canvas, on the page. You begin the work proper. Now you have gone and done it. Now the thing is no longer a vision: it is paper.

Words lead to other words and down the garden path. You adjust the paints' values and hues not to the world, not to the vision, but to the rest of the paint. The materials are stubborn and rigid; push is always coming to shove. You can fly—you can fly higher than you thought possible—but you can never get off the page. After every passage another passage follows, more sentences, more everything on drearily down. Time and materials hound the work; the vision recedes ever farther into the dim realms.

And so you continue the work, and finish it. Probably by now you have been forced to toss the most essential part of the vision. But this is a concern for mere nostalgia now: for before your eyes, and stealing your heart, is this fighting and frail finished product, entirely opaque. You can see nothing through it. It is only itself, a series of well-known passages, some colored paint. Its relationship to the vision that impelled it is the relationship between any energy and any work, anything unchanging to anything temporal.

The work is not the vision itself, certainly. It is not the vision filled in, as if it had been a coloring book. It is not the vision reproduced in time; that were impossible. It is rather a simulacrum and a replacement. It is a golem. You try—you try every time—to reproduce the vision, to let your light so shine before men. But you can only come along with your bushel and hide it.

———

Who will teach me to write? a reader wanted to know.

The page, the page, that eternal blankness, the blankness of eternity which you cover slowly, affirming time's scrawl as a right and your daring as necessity; the page, which you cover woodenly, ruining it, but asserting your freedom and power to act, acknowledging that you ruin everything you touch but touching it nevertheless, because acting is better than being here in mere opacity; the page, which you cover slowly with the crabbed thread of your gut; the page in the purity of its possibilities; the page of your death, against which you pit such flawed excellences as you can muster with all your life's strength: that page will teach you to write.

There is another way of saying this. Aim for the chopping block. If you aim for the wood, you will have nothing. Aim past the wood, aim through the wood; aim for the chopping block.

Chapter Four

To be buried in lava and not turn a hair, it is then a man shows what stuff he is made of.
—BECKETT, *Malone Dies*

SORRY TO TELL YOU A DREAM!

WHAT IS THIS WRITING LIFE? I was living alone in a house, and had set up a study on the first floor. A portable green Smith-Corona typewriter sat on the table against the wall. I made the mistake, or dreamed I made the mistake, of leaving the room.

I was upstairs when I felt the first tremor. The floor wagged under my feet—what was that?—and the picture frames on the wall stirred. The house shook and made noise. There was a pause; I found my face in the dresser mirror, deadpan. When the floor began again to sway, I walked downstairs, thinking I had better get down while the stairway held.

I saw at once that the typewriter was erupting. The old green Smith-Corona typewriter on the table was exploding with fire and ash. Showers of sparks shot out of its caldera—the dark hollow in which the keys lie. Smoke and cinders poured out, noises exploded and spattered, black dense smoke rose up, and a wild, deep fire lighted the whole thing. It shot sparks.

I pulled down the curtains. When I leaned over the typewriter, sparks burnt round holes in my shirt, and fire singed a sleeve. I dragged the rug away from the sparks. In the kitchen I filled a bucket with water and returned to the erupting typewriter. The typewriter did not seem to be flying apart, only erupting. On my face and hands I felt the heat from the caldera. The yellow fire made a fast, roaring noise. The typewriter itself made a rumbling, grinding noise; the table pitched. Nothing seemed to require my bucket of water. The table surface was ruined, of course, but not aflame. After twenty minutes or so, the eruption subsided.

That night I heard more rumblings—weak ones, ever farther apart. The next day I cleaned the typewriter, table, floor, wall, and ceiling. I threw away the burnt shirt. The following day I cleaned the typewriter again—a film of lampblack still coated the caldera—and then it was over. I have had no trouble with it since. Of course, now I know it can happen.

Chapter Five

One cannot be too scrupulous, too sincere, too submissive before nature . . . but one ought to be more or less master of one's model. —CEZANNE

PEOPLE LOVE PRETTY MUCH the same things best. A writer looking for subjects inquires not after what he loves best, but after what he alone loves at all. Strange seizures beset us. Frank Conroy loves his yo-yo tricks, Emily Dickinson her slant of light; Richard Selzer loves the glistening peritoneum, Faulkner the muddy bottom of a little girl's drawers visible when she's up a pear tree. "Each student of the ferns," I read, "will have his own list of plants that for some reason or another stir his emotions."

Why do you never find anything written about that idiosyncratic thought you advert to, about your fascination with something no one else understands? Because it is up to you. There is something you find interesting, for a reason hard to explain. It is hard to explain because you have never read it on any page; there you begin. You were made and set here to give voice to this, your own astonishment. "The most demanding part of living a lifetime as an artist is the strict discipline of forcing oneself to work steadfastly along the nerve of one's own most intimate sensitivity." Anne Truitt, the sculptor, said this. Thoreau said it another way: know your own bone. "Pursue, keep up with, circle round and round your life. . . . Know your own bone: gnaw at it, bury it, unearth it, and gnaw at it still."

Write as if you were dying. At the same time, assume you write for an audience consisting solely of terminal patients. That is, after all, the case. What would you begin writing if you knew you would die soon? What could you say to a dying person that would not enrage by its triviality?

Write about winter in the summer. Describe Norway as Ibsen did, from a desk in Italy; describe Dublin as James Joyce did, from a desk in Paris. Willa Cather wrote her prairie novels in New York City; Mark Twain wrote *Huckleberry Finn* in Hartford, Connecticut. Recently, scholars learned that Walt Whitman rarely left his room.

———

The writer studies literature, not the world. He lives in the world; he cannot miss it. If he has ever bought a hamburger, or taken a commercial airplane flight, he spares his readers a report of his experience. He is careful of what he reads, for that is what he will write. He is careful of what he learns, because that is what he will know.

The writer knows his field—what has been done, what could be done, the limits—the way a tennis player knows the court. And like that expert, he, too, plays the edges. That is where the exhilaration is. He hits up the line. In writing, he can push the edges. Beyond this limit, here, the reader must recoil. Reason balks, poetry snaps; some madness enters, or strain. Now, courageously and carefully, can he enlarge it, can he nudge the bounds? And enclose what wild power?

The body of literature, with its limits and edges, exists outside some people and inside others. Only after the writer lets literature shape her can she perhaps shape literature. In working-class France, when an apprentice got hurt, or when he got tired, the experienced workers said, "It is the trade entering his body." The art must enter the body, too. A painter cannot use paint like glue or screws to fasten down the world. The tubes of paint are like fingers; they work only if, inside the painter, the neural pathways are wide and clear to the brain. Cell by cell, molecule by molecule, atom by atom, part of the brain changes physical shape to accommodate and fit paint.

You adapt yourself, Paul Klee said, to the contents of the paintbox. Adapting yourself to the contents of the paintbox, he said, is more important than nature and its study. The painter, in other words, does not fit the paints to the world. He most certainly does not fit the world to himself. He fits himself to the paint. The self is the servant who bears the paintbox and its inherited contents. Klee called this insight, quite rightly, "an altogether revolutionary new discovery."

———

A well-known writer got collared by a university student who asked, "Do you think I could be a writer?"

"Well," the writer said, "I don't know. . . . Do you like sentences?"

The writer could see the student's amazement. Sentences? Do I like sentences? I am twenty years old and do I like sentences? If he had liked sentences, of course, he could begin, like a joyful painter I knew. I asked him how he came to be a painter. He said, "I liked the smell of the paint."

———

Hemingway studied, as models, the novels of Knut Hamsun and Ivan Turgenev. Isaac Bashevis Singer, as it happened, also chose Hamsun and Turgenev as models. Ralph Ellison studied Hemingway and Gertrude Stein. Thoreau loved Homer; Eudora Welty loved Chekhov. Faulkner described his debt to Sherwood Anderson and Joyce; E. M. Forster, his debt to Jane Austen and Proust. By contrast, if you ask a twenty-one-year-old poet whose poetry he likes, he might say, unblushing, "Nobody's." In his youth, he has not yet understood that poets like poetry, and novelists like novels; he himself likes only the role, the thought of himself in a hat. Rembrandt and Shakespeare, Tolstoy and Gauguin, possessed, I believe, powerful hearts, not powerful wills. They loved the range of materials they used. The work's possibilities excited them; the field's complexities fired their imaginations. The caring suggested the tasks; the tasks suggested the schedules. They learned their fields and then loved them. They worked, respectfully, out of their love and knowledge, and they produced complex bodies of work that endure. Then, and only then, the world flapped at them some sort of hat, which, if they were still living, they ignored as well as they could, to keep at their tasks.

———

It makes more sense to write one big book—a novel or nonfiction narrative—than to write many stories or essays. Into a long, ambitious project you can fit or pour all you possess and learn. A project that takes five years will accumulate those years' inventions and richnesses. Much of those years' reading will feed the work. Further, writing sentences is difficult whatever their subject. It is no less difficult to write sentences in a recipe than sentences in *Moby-Dick*. So you might as well write *Moby-Dick*. Similarly, since every original work requires a unique form, it is more prudent to struggle with the outcome of only one form—that of a long work— than to struggle with the many forms of a collection. Each chapter of a prolonged narrative is problematic too, of course, and the writer undergoes trials as the structure collapses and coheres by turns—but at least the labor is not all on spec. The chapter already has a context: a tone, setting, characters. The work is already off the ground. You must carry the reader along, but you need not, after the first chapters, bear him aloft while performing a series of tricky introductions.

———

Writing every book, the writer must solve two problems: Can it be done? and, Can I do it? Every book has an intrinsic impossibility, which its writer discovers as soon as his first excitement dwindles. The problem is structural; it is insoluble; it is why no one can ever write this book. Complex stories, essays, and poems have this problem, too—the prohibitive structural defect the writer wishes he had never noticed. He writes it in spite of that. He finds ways to minimize the difficulty; he strengthens other virtues; he cantilevers the whole narrative out into thin air, and it holds. And if it can be done, then he can do it, and only he. For there is nothing in the material for this book that suggests to anyone but him alone its possibilities for meaning and feeling.

———

Why are we reading, if not in hope of beauty laid bare, life heightened and its deepest mystery probed? Can the writer isolate and vivify all in experience that most deeply engages our intellects and our hearts? Can the writer renew our hope for literary forms? Why are we reading if not in hope that the writer will magnify and dramatize our days, will illuminate and inspire us with wisdom, courage, and the possibility of meaningfulness, and will press upon our minds the deepest mysteries, so we may feel again their majesty and power? What do we ever know that is higher than that power which, from time to time, seizes our lives, and reveals us startlingly to ourselves as creatures set down here bewildered? Why does death so catch us by surprise, and why love? We still and always want waking. We should amass half dressed in long lines like tribesmen and shake gourds at each other, to wake up; instead we watch television and miss the show.

And if we are reading for these things, why would anyone read books with advertising slogans and brand names in them? Why would anyone write such books? Commercial intrusion has overrun and crushed, like the last glaciation, a humane landscape. The new landscape and its climate put metaphysics on the run. Must writers collaborate? Well, in fact, the novel as a form has only rarely been metaphysical; it usually presents society. The novel often aims to fasten down the spirit of its time, to make a heightened simulacrum of our recognizable world in order to present it shaped and analyzed. This has never seemed to me worth doing, but it is certainly one thing literature has always done. (Any writer draws idiosyncratic boundaries in the field.) Writers attracted to metaphysics can simply ignore the commercial blare, as if it were a radio, or use historical settings, or flee to nonfiction or poetry. Writers might even, with their eyes wide open, redeem the commercial clap-trap from within the novel, using it not just as a quick, cheap, and perfunctory background but—as Updike did in *Rabbit Is Rich*—as part of the world subject to a broad and sanctifying vision.

———

The sensation of writing a book is the sensation of spinning, blinded by love and daring. It is the sensation of rearing and peering from the bent tip of a grassblade, looking for a route. At its absurd worst, it feels like what mad Jacob Boehme, the German mystic, described in his first book. He was writing, incoherently as usual, about the source of evil. The passage will serve as well for the source of books.

"The whole Deity has in its innermost or begin-ning Birth, in the Pith or Kernel, a very tart, terrible *Sharpness,* in which the astringent Quality is very horrible, tart, hard, dark and cold Attraction or Drawing together, like *Winter,* when there is a fierce, bitter cold Frost, when Water is frozen into Ice, and besides is very intolerable."

If you can dissect out the very intolerable, tart, hard, terribly sharp Pith or Kernel, and begin writ-ing the book compressed therein, the sensation changes. Now it feels like alligator wrestling, at the level of the sentence.

This is your life. You are a Seminole alligator

wrestler. Half naked, with your two bare hands, you hold and fight a sentence's head while its tail tries to knock you over. Several years ago in Florida, an alligator wrestler lost. He was grappling with an alligator in a lagoon in front of a paying crowd. The crowd watched the young Indian and the alligator twist belly to belly in and out of the water; after one plunge, they failed to rise. A young writer named Lorne Ladner described it. Bubbles came up on the water. Then blood came up, and the water stilled. As the minutes elapsed, the people in the crowd exchanged glances; silent, helpless, they quit the stands. It took the Indians a week to find the man's remains.

At its best, the sensation of writing is that of any unmerited grace. It is handed to you, but only if you look for it. You search, you break your heart, your back, your brain, and then—and only then—it is handed to you. From the corner of your eye you see motion. Something is moving through the air and headed your way. It is a parcel bound in ribbons and bows; it has two white wings. It flies directly at you; you can read your name on it. If it were a baseball, you would hit it out of the park. It is that one pitch in a thousand you see in slow motion; its wings beat slowly as a hawk's.

One line of a poem, the poet said—only one line, but thank God for that one line—drops from the ceiling. Thornton Wilder cited this unnamed writer of sonnets: one line of a sonnet falls from the ceiling, and you tap in the others around it with a jeweler's hammer. Nobody whispers it in your ear. It is like something you memorized once and forgot. Now it comes back and rips away your breath. You find and finger a phrase at a time; you lay it down cautiously, as if with tongs, and wait suspended until the next one finds you: Ah yes, then this; and yes, praise be, then this.

Einstein likened the generation of a new idea to a chicken's laying an egg: *"Kieks—auf einmal ist es da."* Cheep—and all at once there it is. Of course, Einstein was not above playing to the crowd.

———

One January day, working alone in that freezing borrowed cabin I used for a study on Puget Sound—heated not at all by the alder I chopped every morning—I wrote one of the final passages of a short, difficult book. It was a wildish passage in which the narrator, I, came upon the baptism of Christ in the water of the bay in front of the house. There was a northeaster on—as I wrote. The stormy salt water I saw from the cabin window looked dark as ink. The parallel rows of breakers made lively, broken lines, closely spaced row on row, moving fast and pulling the eyes; they reproduced the sensation of reading exactly, but without reading's sense. Mostly I shut my eyes. I have never been in so trancelike a state, and in fact I dislike, as romantic, the suggestion that any writer works in any peculiar state. I sat motionless with my eyes shut, like a Greek funerary marble.

The writing was simple yet graceless; it surprised me. It was arrhythmical, nonvisual, clunky. It was halting, as if there were no use trying to invoke beauty or power. It was plain and ugly, urgent, like child's talk. "He led him into the water," it said, without antecedents. It read like a translation from the *Gallic Wars*.

Once when I opened my eyes the page seemed bright. The windows were steamed and the sun had gone behind the firs on the bluff. I must have had my eyes closed long. I had been repeating to myself, for hours, like a song, "It is the grave of Jesus, where he lay." From Wallace Stevens' poem, "Sunday Morning." It was three o'clock then; I heated some soup. By the time I left, I was scarcely alive. The way home was along the beach. The beach was bright and distinct. The storm still blew. I was light, dizzy, barely there. I remembered some legendary lamas, who wear chains to keep from floating away. Walking itself seemed to be a stunt; I could not tell whether I was walking fast or slowly. My thighs felt as if they had been reamed.

And I have remembered it often, later, waking up in that cabin to windows steamed blue and the sun gone around the island; remembered putting down those queer, stark sentences half blind on yellow paper; remembered walking ensorcerized, tethered, down the gray cobble beach like an aisle. Evelyn Underhill describes another life, and a better one, in words that recall to me that day, and many another day, at this queer task: "He goes because he must, as Galahad went towards the Grail: knowing that for those who can live it, this alone is life."

———

Push it. Examine all things intensely and relentlessly. Probe and search each object in a piece of art. Do not leave it, do not course over it, as if it were understood, but instead follow it down until you see it in the mystery of its own specificity and strength. Giacometti's drawings and paintings show his bewilderment and persistence. If he had not acknowledged his bewilderment, he would not have persisted. A twentieth-century master of drawing, Rico Lebrun, taught that "the draftsman must aggress; only by persistent assault will the live image capitulate and give up its secret to an unrelenting line." Who but an artist fierce to know—not fierce to seem to know—would suppose that a live image possessed a secret? The artist is willing to give all his or her strength and life to probing with blunt instruments those same secrets no one can describe in any way but with those instruments' faint tracks.

Admire the world for never ending on you—as you would admire an opponent, without taking your eyes from him, or walking away.

One of the few things I know about writing is this: spend it all, shoot it, play it, lose it, all, right away, every time. Do not hoard what seems good for a later place in the book, or for another book; give it, give it all, give it now. The impulse to save something good for a better place later is the signal to spend it now. Something more will arise for later, something better. These things fill from behind, from beneath, like well water. Similarly, the impulse to keep to yourself what you have learned is not only shameful, it is destructive. Anything you do not give freely and abundantly becomes lost to you. You open your safe and find ashes.

After Michelangelo died, someone found in his studio a piece of paper on which he had written a note to his apprentice, in the handwriting of his old age: "Draw, Antonio, draw, Antonio, draw and do not waste time."

Chapter Six

*If this life be not a real fight, in which
something is eternally gained for the universe
by success, it is no better than a game of private
theatricals from which one may withdraw at will.
But it feels like a real fight.* —WILLIAM JAMES

THAT ISLAND on Haro Strait haunts me. The few people there, unconnected to the mainland—lacking ferryboat, electrical cables, and telephone cables—lived lonesome and half mad out in the wind and current like petrels. They had stuck their necks out. In summer they slept in open sleep shacks on the beach. The island lay on the northern edge of the forty-eight states, and on the western edge of the forty-eight states, and was fantastically difficult of access. Once you had gone so far, you might as well test the limits, like an artist playing the edges, and all but sleep in the waves. With my husband, I moved there every summer; we spent a winter there, too. Our cabin on the beach faced west, toward some distant Canadian islands, and Japan.

The waters there were cold and deep; fierce tides

ripped in and out twice a day. The San Juan Islands aggravated tidal currents—they made narrow channels through which enormous volumes of water streamed fast. If an ordinary tide flowed up the beach and caught an oar or a life vest, it swept it northward on the island faster than you could chase it walking alongside; you had to run. The incoming tide ran north; the outgoing tide drained south.

———

Paul Glenn was a painter, a strong-armed, soft-faced, big blond man in his fifties; every summer he lived down the beach. He was a friend of the family. One summer morning I visited him, and asked about his painting. We sat at his kitchen table.

His recent easel painting, and his study of abstract expressionist Mark Tobey's canvases, and his new interest in certain Asian subjects, his understanding of texture in two dimensions, and possibly the mistiness of the Pacific Northwest and its fabulous, busy skies—something, I do not know what, had gotten him experimenting with dipping papers into vats of water on which pools of colored oil floated. He had such papers drying on the kitchen counters. Some of them looked like a book's marbled endpapers, or fine wallpaper—merely decorative. Some others were complex and subtle surfaces, suggestive and powerful. Paul Glenn was learning which techniques of dripping the colors on the water, and which techniques of drawing the paper up through the colors, yielded the interesting results. He had been working at it for six months. How he was going to use the papers was another matter, and the crucial one: he could cut them into collage material, he could fold them into sculpture, he could paint over them and into them. He was following the work wherever it led.

————

The next summer, we returned to the island. Paul Glenn had spent the winter there. I visited him in his house on the beach in late June. He was tan of face already, and perfectly sane—witty and forceful, if a bit soft of voice.

I asked Paul how his work was going.

"You couldn't have known Ferrar Burn," he said. We were sitting at the round table by the kitchen window. There were white shells on the windowsill, and black beach stones. "He died twenty years ago. He was a joyful man, and a calm and determined one. He brought his family out here—June Burn, who wrote books and newspaper columns, and two little boys, you know North and Bob—out here to this island, where there's nothing but what you can find on the beach or grow."

Evidently Paul did not want to talk about how his work was going. Fair enough.

"Ferrar was striking: he had that same pale, thin skin his sons have, and their black eyes and hair. He and June built that cedar shack up on Fishery Point. It was her study. Their house was near the woods— nice timbers."

Paul knew I knew all this, except what Ferrar looked like. Paul's hair had grown long; he kept moving pale strands of it behind his ears. I was fresh from the mainland, a little too bright and quick. He laughed openly at what he could easily see was my impatience; we had been tolerant friends for a few years.

"One evening," he went on, "Ferrar saw a log floating out in the channel. It looked yellow, like Alaska cedar; he hoped it was Alaska cedar. He rowed out to get it."

Everyone on the island scavenged the valuable logs, for building. If the logs did not wash up on the beach, it took a motorboat to get them in; they were heavy in the water.

"It was high tide, slack. Ferrar saw the log, launched his little skiff at Fishery Point, and rowed out in the channel. Sure enough, it was that beautiful Alaska cedar, that pale yellow wood—just a short log, about eight feet, or he never would have tried it without a motor. I guess he thought he could row it in while the tide was still slack.

"He tied onto the log"—such logs often have a big iron staple hammered into one end—"and started rowing back home with it. He had about twenty feet of line on it. He started rowing home, and the tide caught him."

From Paul's window, I could look north up the beach and see Fishery Point. One of Ferrar's sons still used that old rowboat—a little eight-foot pram, now painted yellow and blue. Paul's blue eyes caught mine again.

"The tide started going out, and it caught that log and dragged it south. Ferrar kept rowing back north toward his house. The tide pulled him south down the strait here"—Paul indicated the long sweep of salt water in front of his house—"from one end to the other. Ferrar kept rowing toward Fishery Point. He might as well have tied onto a whale. He was rowing to the north and moving fast to the south. He traveled stern first. He wanted to be going home, so toward home he kept pulling. When the sun set, at about nine o'clock, he'd swept south the length of this beach, rowing north all the way. When the moon rose a few hours later—he told us—he saw he'd swept south past the island altogether and out into the channel between here and Stuart Island. He had been rowing through those dark hours. He continued to row away from Stuart Island and continued to see it get closer.

"Then he felt the tide go slack, and then he felt it coming in again. The current had reversed.

"Ferrar kept rowing in the half moonlight. The tide poured in from the south. He kept rowing north for home—only now the log was with him. He and his log were both floating on the current, and the current was bearing them up and carrying them like platters. It started getting light at about three o'clock, and he rowed back past this island's southern tip. The sun came up, and he rowed all the length of this beach. The tide brought him back on home. His wife, June, saw him coming; she'd been curious about him all night."

Paul had a wide, loose smile. He shifted in his chair. He raised his coffee cup, as if to say, Cheers.

"He pulled up on his own beach. They got the log

rolled beyond the tideline. I saw him a few days later. Everybody knew he'd been carried out almost to Stuart Island, trying to bring in a log. Everybody knew he just kept rowing in the same direction. I asked him about it. He said he had a little backache. I didn't see the palms of his hands."

Paul looked into his empty coffee cup, pleased, and then looked through the window, still smiling. I started to carry my coffee cup to the sink, but he motioned me down. He wasn't finished.

———

"So that's how my work is going," he said.

What?

"You asked how my work is going," he said. "That's how it's going. The current's got me. Feels like I'm about in the middle of the channel now. I just keep at it. I just keep hoping the tide will turn and bring me in."

———

Anthropologist Godfrey Lienhardt describes the animistic understanding of the Dinka tribe in the Sudan. A Dinka believes his own memories and daydreams to be external to himself, as external as the hills, and quick with substance. A man who had been imprisoned in Khartoum named his infant daughter Khartoum in order to placate Khartoum, which seized him from time to time vividly. He believed that as he walked about his village, Khartoum itself, the city with its prison, overwhelmed him with the force of its presence.

So that island haunts me. I was not in prison there, but instead loosed on the shore of vastness. As I walk about this enclosed bay on Cape Cod, or as I scroll down a computer file to a blank screen, then from time to time the skies part ahead of my path, or the luminous photons on the screen revert to infinite randomness, and I balk again on the brink. The irrational haunts the metaphysical. The opposites meet in the looping sky above appearances, or in the dark alley behind appearances, where danger and power duel in a blur.

There was no continental shelf; the island beach dropped to the deep and sandless ocean floor. The water was so cold throughout the year that a man overboard died in ten minutes. Once I saw two twenty-four-man war canoes race across a passage. Forty-eight bare-chested Lummi Indians paddled them, singing. Once I saw phosphorescent seas in a winter storm in front of the cabin; in the black night black seas broke in wild lines to the horizon and spilled green foam that glowed when the wind's pitch rose, so I wept on the shore in fear.

I lived on the beach with one foot in fatal salt water and one foot on a billion grains of sand. The brink of the infinite there was too like writing's solitude. Each sentence hung over an abyssal ocean or sky which held all possibilities, as well as the possibility of nothing. In June and July, the twilight lingered till dawn. Our latitude was north of Nova Scotia; the sun never dropped low enough below the horizon to achieve what is called astronomical night. The wide days split life open like an ax. When

I sketched or painted the island shore, even with the most literal intentions, the work twined into the infinite again and dissolved, or the infinite assaulted the page again and required me to represent it. My pen piled the page with changing clouds, multiple suns, circles, spirals, and rays. I used the pages at night to light fires.

"I have been doing some skying," Constable wrote a friend. I have been doing some scrolling, here and elsewhere, scrolling up and down beaches and blank monitor screens scrying for signs: dipping pens into ink, dipping papers into vats of color, dipping paddles into seas, and bearing God knows where. The green line of photons forms words at the shore of darkness. Darkness empties behind the screen in an illimitable cone. Shall we go rowing again, we who believe we may indeed row off the edge and fall? Shall we launch again into the deep and row up the skies?

Chapter Seven

It's easy, after all, not to be a writer. Most people aren't writers, and very little harm comes to them.
—JULIAN BARNES, *Flaubert's Parrot*

DAVE RAHM lived in Bellingham, Washington, north of Seattle. Bellingham, a harbor town, lies between the San Juan Islands in Haro Strait and the alpine North Cascade Mountains. I lived there between stints on the island. Dave Rahm was a stunt pilot, the air's own genius.

In 1975, with a newcomer's willingness to try anything once, I attended the Bellingham Air Show. The Bellingham airport was a wide clearing in a forest of tall Douglas firs; its runways suited small planes. It was June. People wearing blue or tan zipped jackets stood loosely on the concrete walkways and runways outside the coffee shop. At that latitude in June, you stayed outside because you could, even most of the night, if you could think up something to do. The sky did not darken until ten o'clock or so, and it never got very dark. Your life parted and opened in the sunlight. You tossed your dark winter routines, thought up mad projects, and improvised everything from hour to hour. Being a stunt pilot seemed the most reasonable thing in the world; you could wave your arms in the air all day and all night, and sleep next winter.

———

I saw from the ground a dozen stunt pilots; the air show scheduled them one after the other, for an hour of aerobatics. Each pilot took up his or her plane and performed a batch of tricks. They were precise and impressive. They flew upside down, and straightened out; they did barrel rolls, and straightened out; they drilled through dives and spins, and landed gently on a far runway.

For the end of the day, separated from all other performances of every sort, the air show director had scheduled a program titled "DAVE RAHM." The leaflet said that Rahm was a geologist who taught at Western Washington University. He had flown for King Hussein in Jordan. A tall man in the crowd told me Hussein had seen Rahm fly on a visit the king made to the United States; he had invited him to Jordan to perform at ceremonies. Hussein was a pilot, too. "Hussein thought he was the greatest thing in the world."

Idly, paying scant attention, I saw a medium-sized, rugged man dressed in brown leather, all begoggled, climb in a black biplane's open cockpit. The plane was a Bücker Jungman, built in the thirties. I saw a tall, dark-haired woman seize a propeller tip at the plane's nose and yank it down till the engine caught. He was off; he climbed high over the airport in his biplane, very high until he was barely visible as a mote, and then seemed to fall down the air, diving headlong, and streaming beauty in spirals behind him.

The black plane dropped spinning, and flattened out spinning the other way; it began to carve the air into forms that built wildly and musically on each other and never ended. Reluctantly, I started paying attention. Rahm drew high above the world an inexhaustibly glorious line; it piled over our heads in loops and arabesques. It was like a Saul Steinberg fantasy; the plane was the pen. Like Steinberg's contracting and billowing pen line, the line Rahm spun moved to form new, punning shapes from the edges of the old. Like a Klee line, it smattered the sky with landscapes and systems.

———

The air show announcer hushed. He had been squawking all day, and now he quit. The crowd stilled. Even the children watched dumbstruck as the slow, black biplane buzzed its way around the air. Rahm made beauty with his whole body; it was pure pattern, and you could watch it happen. The plane moved every way a line can move, and it controlled three dimensions, so the line carved massive and subtle slits in the air like sculptures. The plane looped the loop, seeming to arch its back like a gymnast; it stalled, dropped, and spun out of it climbing; it spiraled and knifed west on one side's wings and back east on another; it turned cartwheels, which must be physically impossible; it played with its own line like a cat with yarn. How did the pilot know where in the air he was? If he got lost, the ground would swat him.

Rahm did everything his plane could do: tailspins, four-point rolls, flat spins, figure 8's, snap rolls, and hammerheads. He did pirouettes on the plane's tail. The other pilots could do these stunts, too, skillfully, one at a time. But Rahm used the plane inexhaustibly, like a brush marking thin air.

His was pure energy and naked spirit. I have thought about it for years. Rahm's line unrolled in time. Like music, it split the bulging rim of the future along its seam. It pried out the present. We watchers waited for the split-second curve of beauty in the present to reveal itself. The human pilot, Dave Rahm, worked in the cockpit right at the plane's nose; his very body tore into the future for us and reeled it down upon us like a curling peel.

Like any fine artist, he controlled the tension of the audience's longing. You desired, unwittingly, a certain kind of roll or climb, or a return to a certain portion of the air, and he fulfilled your hope slantingly, like a poet, or evaded it until you thought you would burst, and then fulfilled it surprisingly, so you gasped and cried out.

The oddest, most exhilarating and exhausting thing was this: he never quit. The music had no periods, no rests or endings; the poetry's beautiful sentence never ended; the line had no finish; the sculptured forms piled overhead, one into another without surcease. Who could breathe, in a world where rhythm itself had no periods?

It had taken me several minutes to understand what an extraordinary thing I was seeing. Rahm kept all that embellished space in mind at once. For another twenty minutes I watched the beauty unroll and grow more fantastic and unlikely before my eyes. Now Rahm brought the plane down slidingly, and just in time, for I thought I would snap from the effort to compass and remember the line's long intelligence; I could not add another curve. He brought the plane down on a far runway. After a pause, I saw him step out, an ordinary man, and make his way back to the terminal.

———

The show was over. It was late. Just as I turned from the runway, something caught my eye and made me laugh. It was a swallow, a blue-green swallow, having its own air show, apparently inspired by Rahm. The swallow climbed high over the runway, held its wings oddly, tipped them, and rolled down the air in loops. The inspired swallow. I always want to paint, too, after I see the Rembrandts. The blue-green swallow tumbled precisely, and caught itself and flew up again as if excited, and looped down again, the way swallows do, but tensely, holding its body carefully still. It was a stunt swallow.

———

I went home and thought about Rahm's performance that night, and the next day, and the next.

I had thought I knew my way around beauty a little bit. I knew I had devoted a good part of my life to it, memorizing poetry and focusing my attention on complexity of rhythm in particular, on force, movement, repetition, and surprise, in both poetry and prose. Now I had stood among dandelions between two asphalt runways in Bellingham, Washington, and begun learning about beauty. Even the Boston Museum of Fine Arts was never more inspiriting than this small northwestern airport on this time-killing Sunday afternoon in June. Nothing on earth is more gladdening than knowing we must roll up our sleeves and move back the boundaries of the humanly possible once more.

———

Later I flew with Dave Rahm; he took me up. A generous geographer, Dick Smith, at Western Washington University, arranged it, and came along. Rahm and Dick Smith were colleagues at the university. In geology, Rahm had published two books and many articles. Rahm was handsome in a dull sort of way, blunt-featured, wide-jawed, wind-burned, keen-eyed, and taciturn. As anyone would expect. He was forty. He wanted to show me the Cascade Mountains; these enormous peaks, only fifty miles from the coast, rise over nine thousand feet; they are heavily glaciated. Whatcom County has more glaciers than the lower forty-eight states combined; the Cascades make the Rocky Mountains look like hills. Mount Baker is volcanic, like most Cascade peaks. That year, Mount Baker was acting up. Even from my house at the shore I could see, early in the morning on clear days, volcanic vapor rise near its peak. Often the vapor made a cloud which swelled all morning and hid the snows. Every day the newspapers reported on Baker's activity: would it blow? (A few years later, Mount St. Helens did blow.)

Rahm was not flying his trick biplane that day, but a faster, enclosed plane, a single-engine Cessna. We flew from a bumpy grass airstrip near my house, out over the coast and inland. There was coastal plain down there, but we could not see it for clouds. We were over the clouds at five hundred feet and inside them too, heading for an abrupt line of peaks we could not see. I gave up on everything, the way you do in airplanes; it was out of my hands. Every once in a while Rahm saw a peephole in the clouds and buzzed over for a look. "That's Larsen's pea farm," he said, or "That's Nooksack Road," and he changed our course with a heave.

When we got to the mountains, he slid us along Mount Baker's flanks sideways.

Our plane swiped at the mountain with a roar. I glimpsed a windshield view of dirty snow traveling fast. Our shaking, swooping belly seemed to graze the snow. The wings shuddered; we peeled away and the mountain fell back and the engines whined. We felt flung, because we were in fact flung; parts of our faces and internal organs trailed pressingly behind on the curves. We came back for another pass at the mountain, and another. We dove at the snow headlong like suicides; we jerked up, down, or away at the last second, so late we left our hearts, stomachs, and lungs behind. If I forced myself to hold my heavy head up against the g's, and to raise my eyelids, heavy as barbells, and to notice what I saw, I could see the wrinkled green crevasses cracking the glaciers' snow.

Pitching snow filled all the windows, and shapes of dark rock. I had no notion which way was up. Everything was black or gray or white except the fatal crevasses; everything made noise and shook. I felt my face smashed sideways and saw rushing abstractions of snow in the windshield. Patches of cloud obscured the snow fleetingly. We straightened out, turned, and dashed at the mountainside for another pass, which we made, apparently, on our ear, an inch or two away from the slope. Icefalls and cornices jumbled and fell away. If a commercial plane's black box, such as the FAA painstakingly recovers from crash sites, could store videotapes as well as pilots' last words, some videotapes would look like this: a mountainside coming up at the windows from all directions, ice and snow and rock filling the screen up close and screaming by.

Rahm was just being polite. His geographer colleague wanted to see the fissure on Mount Baker from which steam escaped. Everybody in Bellingham wanted to see that sooty fissure, as did every geologist in the country; no one on earth could fly so close to it as Rahm. He knew the mountain by familiar love and feel, like a face; he knew what the plane could do and what he dared to do.

When Mount Baker inexplicably let us go, he jammed us into cloud again and soon tilted. "The Sisters!" someone shouted, and I saw the windshield fill with red rock. This mountain looked infernal, a drear and sheer plane of lifeless rock. It was red and sharp; its gritty blades cut through the clouds at random. The mountain was quiet. It was in shade. Careening, we made sideways passes at these brittle peaks too steep for snow. Their rock was full of iron, somebody shouted at me then or later; the iron had rusted, so they were red. Later, when I was back on the ground, I recalled that, from a distance, the two jagged peaks called the Twin Sisters looked translucent against the sky; they were sharp, tapered, and fragile as arrowheads.

I talked to Rahm. He was flying us out to the islands now. The islands were fifty or sixty miles away. Like many other people, I had picked Bellingham, Washington, by looking at an atlas. It was clear from the atlas that you could row in the salt water and see snow-covered mountains; you could scale a glaciated mountainside with an ice ax in August, skirting green crevasses two hundred feet deep, and look out on the islands in the sea. Now, in the air, the clouds had risen over us; dark forms lay on the glinting water. There was almost no color to the day, just blackened green and some yellow. I knew the islands were forested in dark Douglas firs the size of skyscrapers. Bald eagles scavenged on the beaches; robins the size of herring gulls sang in the clearings. We made our way out to the islands through the layer of air between the curving planet and its held, thick clouds.

"When I started trying to figure out what I was going to do with my life, I decided to become an expert on mountains. It wasn't much to be, it wasn't everything, but it was something. I was going to know everything about mountains from every point of view. So I started out in geography." Geography proved too pedestrian for Rahm, too concerned with "how many bushels of wheat an acre." So he ended up in geology. Smith had told me that geology departments throughout the country used Rahm's photographic slides—close-ups of geologic features from the air.

"I used to climb mountains. But you know, you can get a better feel for a mountain's power flying around it, flying all around it, than you can from climbing it tied to its side like a flea."

He talked about his flying performances. He thought of the air as a line, he said. "This end of the line, that end of the line—like a rope." He improvised. "I get a rhythm going and stick with it." While he was performing in a show, he paid attention, he said, to the lighting. He didn't play against the sun. That was all he said about what he did.

In aerobatic maneuvers, pilots pull about seven positive g's on some stunts and six negative g's on others. Some gyrations push; others pull. Pilots alternate the pressures carefully, so they do not gray out or black out.

Later I learned that some stunt pilots tune up by wearing gravity boots. These are boots made to hook over a doorway; wearing them, you hang in the doorway upside-down. It must startle a pilot's children, to run into their father or mother in the course of their home wanderings—the parent hanging wide-eyed upside-down in the doorway like a bat.

We were landing; here was the airstrip on Stuart Island—that island to which Ferrar Burn was dragged by the tide. We put down, climbed out of the plane, and walked. We wandered a dirt track through fields to a lee shore where yellow sandstone ledges slid into the sea. The salt chuck, people there called salt water. The sun came out. I caught a snake in the salt chuck; the snake, eighteen inches long, was swimming in the green shallows.

———

I had a survivor's elation. Rahm had found Mount Baker in the clouds before Mount Baker found the plane. He had wiped it with the fast plane like a cloth and we had lived. When we took off from Stuart Island and gained altitude, I asked if we could turn over—could we do a barrel roll? The plane was making a lot of noise, and Dick Smith did not hear any of this, I learned later. "Why not?" Rahm said, and added surprisingly, "It won't hurt the plane." Without ado he leaned on the wheel and the wing went down and we went somersaulting over it. We upended with a roar. We stuck to the plane's sides like flung paint. All the blood in my body bulged on my face; it piled between my skull and skin. Vaguely I could see the chrome sea twirling over Rahm's head like a baton, and the dark islands sliding down the skies like rain.

The g's slammed me into my seat like thugs and pinned me while my heart pounded and the plane turned over slowly and compacted each organ in turn. My eyeballs were newly spherical and full of heartbeats. I seemed to hear a crescendo; the wing rolled shuddering down the last ninety degrees and settled on the flat. There were the islands, admirably below us, and the clouds, admirably above. When I could breathe, I asked if we could do it again, and we did. He rolled the other way. The brilliant line of the sea slid up the side window bearing its heavy islands. Through the shriek of my blood and the plane's shakes I glimpsed the line of the sea over the windshield, thin as a spear. How in performance did Rahm keep track while his brain blurred and blood roared in his ears without ceasing? Every performance was a tour de force and a show of will, a *machtspruch.* I had seen the other stunt pilots straighten out after a trick or two; their blood could drop back and the planet simmer down. An Olympic gymnast, at peak form, strings out a line of spins ten stunts long across a mat, and is hard put to keep his footing at the end. Rahm endured much greater pressure on his faster spins using the plane's power, and he could spin in three dimensions and keep twirling till he ran out of sky room or luck.

When we straightened out, and had flown straightforwardly for ten minutes toward home, Dick Smith, clearing his throat, brought himself to speak. "What was that we did out there?"

"The barrel rolls?" Rahm said. "They were barrel rolls." He said nothing else. I looked at the back of his head; I could see the serious line of his cheek and jaw. He was in shirtsleeves, tanned, strong-wristed. I could not imagine loving him under any circumstance; he was alien to me, unfazed. He looked like G.I. Joe. He flew with that matter-of-fact, bored gesture pilots use. They click overhead switches and turn dials as if only their magnificent strength makes such dullness endurable. The half circle of wheel in their big hands looks like a toy they plan to crush in a minute; the wiggly stick the wheel mounts seems barely attached.

A crop-duster pilot in Wyoming told me the life expectancy of a crop-duster pilot is five years. They fly too low. They hit buildings and power lines. They have no space to fly out of trouble, and no space to recover from a stall. We were in Cody, Wyoming, out on the North Fork of the Shoshone River. The crop duster had wakened me that morning flying over the ranch house and clearing my bedroom roof by half an inch. I saw the bolts on the wheel assembly a few feet from my face. He was spraying with pesticide the plain old grass. Over breakfast I asked him how long he had been dusting crops. "Four years," he said, and the figure stalled in the air between us for a moment. "You know you're going to die at it someday," he added. "We all know it. We accept that; it's part of it." I think now that, since the crop duster was in his twenties, he accepted only that he had to say such stuff; privately he counted on skewing the curve.

I suppose Rahm knew the fact, too. I do not know how he felt about it. "It's worth it," said the early French aviator Mermoz. He was Antoine de Saint-Exupéry's friend. "It's worth the final smashup."

Rahm smashed up in front of King Hussein, in Jordan, during a performance. The plane spun down and never came out of it; it nosedived into the ground and exploded. He bought the farm. I was living then with my husband out on that remote island in the San Juans, cut off from everything. Battery radios picked up the Canadian Broadcasting Company out of Toronto, half a continent away; island people would, in theory, learn if the United States blew up, but not much else. There were no newspapers. One friend got the Sunday *New York Times* by mailboat on the following Friday. He saved it until Sunday and had a party, every week; we all read the Sunday *Times* and no one mentioned that it was last week's.

One day, Paul Glenn's brother flew out from Bellingham to visit; he had a seaplane. He landed in the water in front of the cabin and tied up to our mooring. He came in for coffee, and he gave out news of this and that, and—Say, did we know that stunt pilot Dave Rahm had cracked up? In Jordan, during a performance: he never came out of a dive. He just dove right down into the ground, and his wife was there watching. "I saw it on CBS News last night." And then—with a sudden sharp look at my filling eyes—"What, did you know him?" But no, I did not know him. He took me up once. Several years ago. I admired his flying. I had thought that danger was the safest thing in the world, if you went about it right.

Later I found a newspaper. Rahm was living in Jordan that year; King Hussein invited him to train the aerobatics team, the Royal Jordanian Falcons. He was also visiting professor of geology at the University of Jordan. In Amman that day he had been flying a Pitt Special, a plane he knew well. Katy Rahm, his wife of six months, was sitting beside Hussein in the viewing stands, with her daughter. Rahm died performing a Lomcevak combined with a tail slide and hammerhead. In a Lomcevak, the pilot brings the plane up on a slant and pirouettes. I had seen Rahm do this: the falling plane twirled slowly like a leaf. Like a ballerina, the plane seemed to hold its head back stiff in concentration at the music's slow, painful beauty. It was one of Rahm's favorite routines. Next the pilot flies straight up, stalls the plane, and slides down the air on his tail. He brings the nose down—the hammerhead—kicks the engine, and finishes with a low loop.

It is a dangerous maneuver at any altitude, and Rahm was doing it low. He hit the ground on the loop; the tail slide had left him no height. When

Rahm went down, King Hussein dashed to the burning plane to pull him out, but he was already dead.

———

A few months after the air show, and a month after I had flown with Rahm, I was working at my desk near Bellingham, where I lived, when I heard a sound so odd it finally penetrated my concentration. It was the buzz of an airplane, but it rose and fell musically, and it never quit; the plane never flew out of earshot. I walked out on the porch and looked up: it was Rahm in the black and gold biplane, looping all over the air. I had been wondering about his performance flight: could it really have been so beautiful? It was, for here it was again. The little plane twisted all over the air like a vine. It trailed a line like a very long mathematical proof you could follow only so far, and then it lost you in its complexity. I saw Rahm flying high over the Douglas firs, and out over the water, and back over farms. The air was a fluid, and Rahm was an eel.

It was as if Mozart could move his body through his notes, and you could walk out on the porch, look up, and see him in periwig and breeches, flying around in the sky. You could hear the music as he dove through it; it streamed after him like a contrail.

I lost myself; standing on the firm porch, I lost my direction and reeled. My neck and spine rose and turned, so I followed the plane's line kinesthetically. In his open-cockpit, black plane, Rahm demonstrated curved space. He slid down ramps of air, he vaulted and wheeled. He piled loops in heaps and praised height. He unrolled the scroll of the air, extended it, and bent it into Möbius strips; he furled line in a thousand new ways, as if he were inventing a script and writing it in one infinitely recurving utterance until I thought the bounds of beauty must break.

From inside, the looping plane had sounded tinny, like a kazoo. Outside, the buzz rose and fell to the Doppler effect as the plane looped near or away. Rahm cleaved the sky like a prow and tossed out time left and right in his wake. He performed for forty minutes; then he headed the plane, as small as a wasp, back to the airport inland. Later I learned Rahm often practiced acrobatic flights over this shore. His idea was that if he lost control and was going to go down, he could ditch in the salt chuck, where no one else would get hurt.

─────

If I had not turned two barrel rolls in an airplane, I might have fancied Rahm felt good up there, and playful. Maybe Jackson Pollock felt a sort of playfulness, in addition to the artist's usual deliberate and intelligent care. In my limited experience, painting, unlike writing, pleases the senses while you do it, and more while you do it than after it is done. Drawing lines with an airplane, unfortunately, tortures the senses. Jet bomber pilots black out. I knew Rahm felt as if his brain were bursting his eardrums, felt that if he let his jaws close as tight as centrifugal force pressed them, he would bite through his lungs.

"All virtue is a form of acting," Yeats said. Rahm deliberately turned himself into a figure. Sitting invisible at the controls of a distant airplane, he became the agent and the instrument of art and invention. He did not tell me how he felt, when we spoke of his performance flying; he told me instead that he paid attention to how his plane and its line looked to the audience against the lighted sky. If he had noticed how he felt, he could not have done the work. Robed in his airplane, he was as featureless as a priest. He was lost in his figural aspect like an actor or a king. Of his flying, he had said only, "I get a rhythm and stick with it." In its reticence, this statement reminded me of Veronese's "Given a large canvas, I enhanced it as I saw fit." But Veronese was ironic, and Rahm was not; he was literal as an astronaut; the machine gave him tongue.

When Rahm flew, he sat down in the middle of art, and strapped himself in. He spun it all around him. He could not see it himself. If he never saw it on film, he never saw it at all—as if Beethoven could not hear his final symphonies not because he was deaf, but because he was inside the paper on which he wrote. Rahm must have felt it happen, that fusion of vision and metal, motion and idea. I think of this man as a figure, a college professor with a Ph.D. upside down in the loud band of beauty. What are we here for? *Propter chorum,* the monks say: for the sake of the choir.

"Purity does not lie in separation from but in deeper penetration into the universe," Teilhard de Chardin wrote. It is hard to imagine a deeper penetration into the universe than Rahm's last dive in his plane, or than his inexpressible wordless selfless line's inscribing the air and dissolving. Any other art may be permanent. I cannot recall one Rahm sequence. He improvised. If Christo wraps a building or dyes a harbor, we join his poignant and fierce awareness that the work will be gone in days. Rahm's plane shed a ribbon in space, a ribbon whose end unraveled in memory while its beginning unfurled as surprise. He may have acknowledged that what he did could be called art, but it would have been, I think, only in the common misusage, which holds art to be the last extreme of skill. Rahm rode the point of the line to the possible; he discovered it and wound it down to show. He made his dazzling probe on the run. "The world is filled, and filled with the Absolute," Teilhard de Chardin wrote. "To see this is to be made free."

ABOUT THE AUTHOR

ANNIE DILLARD is the author of many works of nonfiction, including *Pilgrim at Tinker Creek* and *An American Childhood*, as well as the novels *The Living* and *The Maytrees*.

BOOKS BY
ANNIE DILLARD

AN AMERICAN CHILDHOOD
Available in Paperback and eBook

"Dillard's '50s childhood in Pittsburgh . . . consumes you as you consume it, so that, when you have put down this book, you're a different person, one who has virtually experienced another childhood." —*The Chicago Tribune*

AN ANNIE DILLARD READER
Available in Paperback and eBook

"One of the most distinctive voices in American letters today" (*The Boston Globe*) collects her favorite selections from her own writings in this compact volume. A perfect introduction to one of America's most acclaimed and bestselling authors.

HOLY THE FIRM
Available in Paperback and eBook

A profound book about the natural world—in both its beauty and its cruelty.

"A book of great richness, beauty, and power. . . . Nature seen so clear and hard that the eyes tear." —*The New York Times Book Review*

LIVING BY FICTION
Available in Paperback and eBook

"A stimulating book, one of those in which quality of thought and felicity of prose seem consequences of one another." —*The New York Times Book Review*

THE LIVING
A Novel

Available in Paperback and eBook

This *New York Times* bestselling novel is a mesmerizing evocation of life in the Pacific Northwest during the last decades of the 19th century.

"An august celebration of human frenzy and endurance and . . . an invigorating, intricate first novel. Annie Dillard shows a tremendous gift for writing in a genuinely epic mode." —*The New York Times Book Review*

THE MAYTREES
A Novel

Available in Paperback and eBook

"The novel as a whole is beautiful, and the beauty is never digressive or ornamental. . . . This is where Dillard's imagination has always lived, in the stark and lyrical awareness of the profundity of the physical world."
—*The Washington Post Book World*

MODERN AMERICAN MEMOIRS
Available in Paperback and eBook

"[In] this anthology of well-chosen excerpts by a satisfyingly diverse group
of writers . . . the truth of their lives shines from every beautifully, often
courageously composed page." —*Booklist*

MORNINGS LIKE THIS
Found Poems
Available in Paperback and eBook

Annie Dillard extracts and rearranges sentences from old (and often odd)
books, and composes ironic poems—some serious, some light—on the heartfelt
themes of love, nature, nostalgia, and death.

PILGRIM AT TINKER CREEK
Available in Paperback and eBook

Winner of the 1975 Pulitzer Prize

"Not only a habitat of cruelty and 'the waste of pain,' but the savage and
magnificent world of the Old Testament, presided over by a passionate
Jehovah with no Messiah in sight. . . . A remarkable psalm of terror and
celebration." —Melvin Maddocks, *Time*

TEACHING A STONE TO TALK
Expeditions and Encounters
Available in Paperback and eBook

"This little book is haloed and informed throughout by Dillard's distinctive
passion and intensity, a sort of intellectual radiance that reminds me of both
Thoreau and Emily Dickinson." —Edward Abbey, *The Chicago Sun-Times*

THREE BY ANNIE DILLARD
The Writing Life, An American Childhood, Pilgrim at Tinker Creek
Available in Paperback

A stunning collection of Annie Dillard's most popular books in one volume.

THE WRITING LIFE
Available in Paperback and eBook

"For nonwriters, it is a glimpse into the trials and satisfactions of a life
spent with words. For writers, it is a warm, rambling, conversation with a
stimulating and extraordinarily talented colleague." —*The Chicago Tribune*

Available wherever books are sold.

HARPER ● PERENNIAL